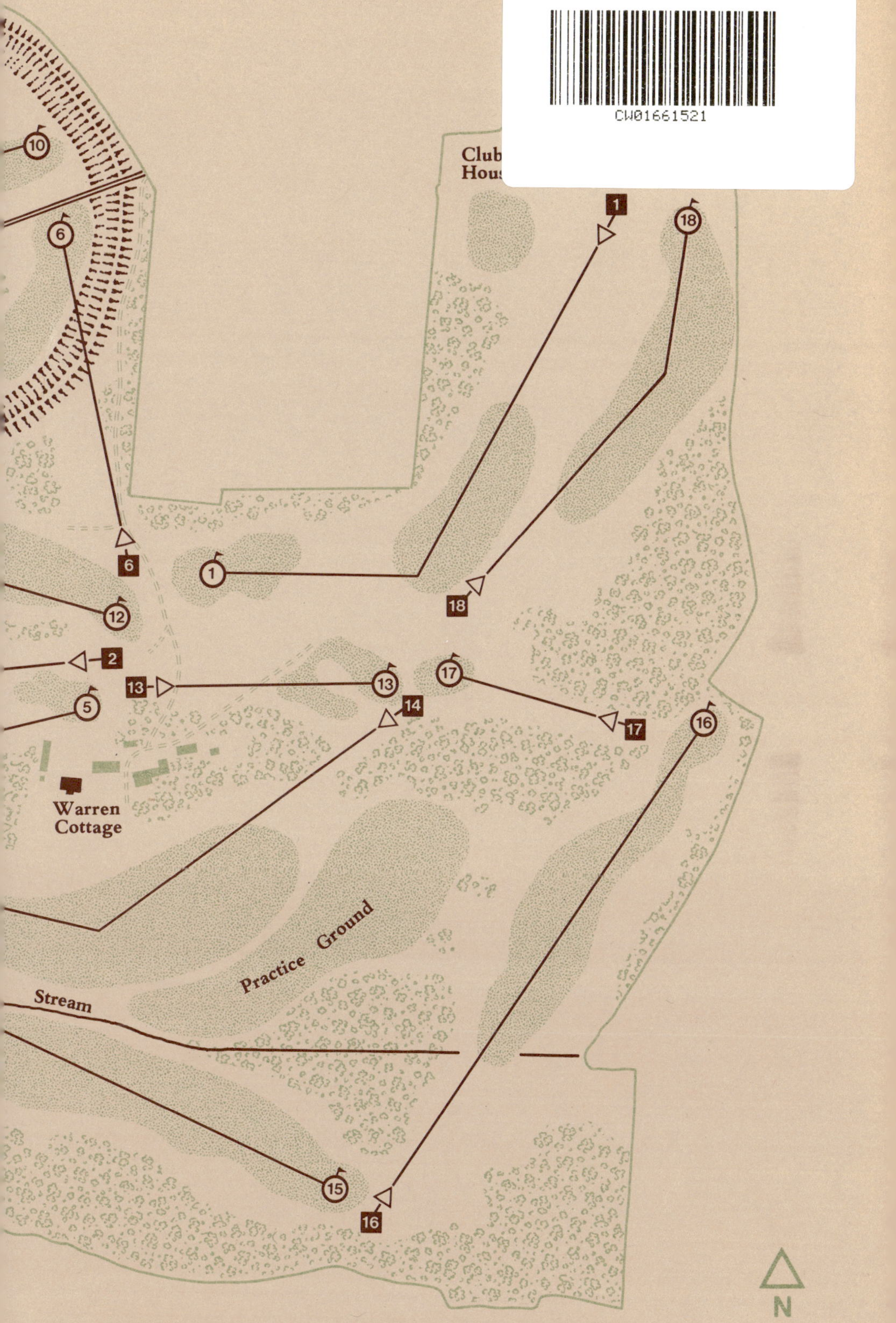
Club
Hous
1
18
10
6
1
18
12
2
13
13
17
14
17
5
16
Warren
Cottage
Practice Ground
Stream
15
16
N

John Flower
Cartographer

The History of
ROYAL WIMBLEDON GOLF CLUB
1865-1986

Charles Cruickshank

Frontispiece
Portrait of Henry Lamb
Honorary Secretary of Royal
Wimbledon Golf Club 1877–90, Captain 1890–91:
by John Pettie RA.

Published 1986 by Royal Wimbledon Golf Club

ISBN 0 00 258118 3

Printed and bound in Great Britain

Contents

PREFACE

THIS FASCINATING BOOK would not have been written but for the inspiration and determination of Stanley Harding (Captain, 1984–85). It is only as a quirk of fate in the timing of its publication that I have the privilege of writing a preface and the pleasure of acknowledging the indebtedness of Royal Wimbledon to those whose individual skills and unstinted efforts were combined to achieve its publication.

Twenty one years have elapsed since the Club celebrated its Centenary. Stanley Harding was inspired with the thought that many of its present Members, and even more in the future, will be interested to learn something about the history of a Club of such character. The project required research, an author, a photographer and a publisher. All the essential skills could be found within the Club, whose membership includes men of distinction in every walk of life. Such is the "Royal Wimbledon spirit" that whenever help is wanted the right man is always ready and willing to devote his talents to the needs of the Club.

I would like to mention first E. C. 'Bunny' Millard, a Member since 1920 – more than half the life of the Club, who has always been a golfer of great distinction and whose recollection of the predecessor of our present Course has been invaluable. He has painstakingly read through all the Minute Books, a task which would have daunted many a younger man.

We are indeed fortunate to have in the Club an historian and author of the calibre of Charles Cruickshank. He is well known for his sixteenth and twentieth century military histories, the latter including several official histories. In this book his puckish sense of humour shines through the text with the clear message that we must not take ourselves too seriously. The affection with which he regards the Club is clear not only from the book but also from the many hours which he has so generously devoted to every aspect of its preparation.

Many of the illustrations are from photographs by Ken Onwood, to whom

I express our sincere gratitude for putting his expertise and time at the disposal of the Club.

Our thanks, too, are due to Ian Chapman, Chairman of William Collins, who has taken a personal interest in the preparation and publication of this book. He has given us the benefit of much helpful advice, for which we are profoundly grateful, as we are to the many unseen hands in William Collins who have shared in the production of the book.

Our thanks are also due to those outside the Club who have readily given assistance. In particular, the Historian of the Royal and Ancient Golf Club, Bobby Burnet, has provided much useful material. The Wimbledon Common Conservators and London Scottish Golf Club have kindly given access to their Minutes.

Royal Wimbledon Golf Club is now in fine fettle. It has deep and strong roots. All the signs suggest that the 300-year lease negotiated during Stanley Harding's year as Captain will prove to have been not a day too long.

Barry Sheen, Captain, 1985–86

Lord Elcho (later Earl of Weymss and March) first President of the Club, who played golf into his 93rd year.

One

ORIGINS

WE DO NOT KNOW when golf began.

One day there will be discovered in North Britain caves adorned with paintings of kilted figures driving balls of polished granite with clubs fashioned from the femurs of defunct dinosaurs. For the moment we must be content with the knowledge that much later James VI played the game and that in 1603 James I brought it south. We are indebted to his colleague Henri IV for the opinion that James was the wisest fool in Christendom; and golfers at large, as they struggle round on Medal Day, may well consider themselves rivals to that title.

It follows that golf was played in England long before it reached Wimbledon Common, first by James's courtiers, who by some quirk of geography found their way to Blackheath rather than Wimbledon, and then elsewhere by lesser mortals. The Scottish influence persisted. When in 1758 Alexander Carlyle, Minister of Inveresk near Edinburgh, was invited by the actor David Garrick to dine at Hampton he was told to bring his golf clubs

> that we might play at that game on Molesly Hurst. We accordingly set out in good time, six of us in a landau. As we passed through Kensington the Coldstream Regiment were changing guard, and on seeing our clubs they gave us three cheers in honour of a diversion peculiar to Scotland ... Immediately after we arrived we crossed to the golfing ground which was very good.

Not content with exhibiting his prowess on the formal Course, Carlyle showed off at Garrick's house while the meal was prepared. His host

> had built a handsome temple with a statue of Shakespeare in it, in his lower garden, on the banks of the Thames, which was separated from the upper one by a high road, under which there was an archway which united the gardens ... Having observed a green mount in the garden, opposite the archway, I said to our landlord [ie Garrick] ... I would surprise him with a stroke at the golf, as I should drive a ball through his archway into the Thames once in three strokes.

He failed with his first shot, but the second whistled through the archway, rolled down the lawn and duly disappeared into the Thames. Garrick was astonished. He asked his guest to present him with the club, perhaps hoping later to emulate the feat. Like every good conjuror, Carlyle did not attempt the trick again.

Golf in Scotland continued to progress, and by 1771, thirteen years after Carlyle uncharacteristically sacrificed a golf ball, the Nineteenth and most essential hole was invented. The authority for this milestone is Tobias Smollett, who recorded

> ... in the fields called the Links, the citizens of Edinburgh divert themselves at a game called golf in which they use a curious kind of bats, tipt with horn, and small elastic balls of leather, stuffed with feathers, rather less than tennis balls, but of a much harder consistence. This they strike with such force and dexterity from one hole to another that they will fly to an incredible distance ... Among others I was shown one particular set of golfers, the youngest of whom was turned of fourscore. They were all gentlemen of independent fortune who had amused themselves with this pastime for the best part of a century, without having ever felt the least alarm from sickness; and they never went to bed without having each the best part of a gallon of claret in his belly.

If golf was played at Blackheath in the seventeenth century and at Hampton in the eighteenth, it was probably played, at least by individuals, on Wimbledon Common in the early nineteenth. It was certainly in the minds of some who used the Common. On 5 November 1864 after a shooting match – Wimbledon Common was the Bisley of the day, headquarters of the National Rifle Association since 1860 – some members of the London Scottish Rifle Volunteers met 'to arrange for a Golf Club'. This is recorded on a fragile page pasted into a later Minute Book of the London Scottish Golf Club; and confirms that the new Club was a going concern in 1865. There is no entry for that year in the fragmentary record, the next being: '1866. Regimental Order of 2 May 1866. The CO [Lord Elcho, later Earl of Wemyss and March] has sanctioned a "London Scottish" Golf Club, and has appointed the following Committee:

Private A. G. Mackenzie
Lieut. R. Fisher
Private Dudgeon MD
[Henry] Usher
Armourer Sergeant J. Kerr Treas.
Ex officio, CO and Adjutant

'Subscription is 5s.0d. a year and will be paid on [page torn] each year'.

The only other entries are the names of the 1867 Committee; a note that the golf match against the Blackheath Club will take place on Saturday 7 December 1867; the dates for the monthly challenge medal competition in February-May 1868; that the Elcho and Hope Grant Medal was won in 1868 by Private Cheyne; and that the result of the monthly medal in November 1867 was:

Private Cheyne 53 strokes
Lieut. Col. Lord Elcho 62
Private Somerville 62
Armourer Sergeant J. Kerr 62
Ensign Porteous 63

The original Golf Course was laid out with the permission of the 5th Earl of Spencer, who held manorial rights over Wimbledon Common. In 1871 these rights were transferred by Act of Parliament to a Board of Conservators elected by ratepayers in the neighbourhood, which became responsible for the management of the Common, and its use for the playing of games, including golf. Until 1871 the golfers had been able to do more or less as they pleased. Now they had to conform to the wishes of the Conservators, and pay closer attention to the rights of other users of the Common.

It was not until 1878 that suitable provision was made for the Nineteenth Hole. The Secretary was directed to keep at the Iron House [local headquarters of the London Scottish Rifle Volunteers, where since 1871 a room had been used as a golf Clubhouse] sherry and whisky to be supplied at 4d. a glass for sherry and 2d. for whisky. Earlier an application for a licence to sell spirits, at which the Conservators raised their eyebrows, was hastily withdrawn by Lord Elcho who said it had been made without his knowledge; but now, licensed or unlicensed, the Club had everything needed for a long, prosperous, and comfortable existence: a challenging, natural golf course, Members dedicated to the game, and a well-stocked bar.

Two

DISSENSIONS

ORIGINALLY the Club on the Common was restricted to members and honorary members of the London Scottish Rifle Volunteers; but they were too few to make a viable Club. In 1869 the admission of Officers of the Army, Navy, Militia, Yeomanry, members of other golf clubs, and residents within three miles of Wimbledon Windmill was approved. Even this larger group was not enough to keep the Club solvent, and the annual subscription was increased from 5s.0d. to 10s.0d. In 1871 the subscription had to be raised again – to a guinea, with a guinea entrance fee. Lord Elcho said if a guinea was essential, he would pay it; but any Corps member pleading poverty [deleted in the Minutes] need pay only 10s.0d. A higher subscription 'would alienate the Club from the Corps, to which it ought to be intimately bound'.

Elcho's word was law. A General Meeting dutifully decided that while economics implied a guinea subscription, members of the Corps need pay no more than 10s.0d. 'should they think fit'. This meant the Club must look elsewhere for subscription income. So the 'Windmill and three miles round rule' was abolished. The Club was opened to 'all outsiders'.

Members of the Corps had an automatic right of entry. Civilians had to face a ballot, although it was seldom called for. The Committee almost invariably accepted nomination and seconding as proof that the candidate would fit in. Corps members had other privileges. If they subscribed to the Armoury lavatory they had free use of the corresponding facility in the Club, for which the civilians paid 2s.6d. a year. They were, however, liable for the going rate for boot cleaning – also 2s.6d. a year, or 1d. a brush.

In 1872 the entrance fee for non-members of the Corps was doubled to two guineas, and two years later it was raised to four. Throwing the Club open to all comers inevitably changed the balance of power. The number of Corps members remained at 50, while the civilians increased to 250. Not only were the Corps members subsidised by the civilians, since their subscription remained at 10s.0d., but the Club management was in the hands of the Corps, which under the early constitution provided the whole Committee. The increase in the number of civilian members, and the uncompromising nature of the Commanding Officer made trouble inevitable. Lord Elcho did not recognize the democratic principle of one man one vote (or he may have believed that one rifleman was worth ten civilians). Well before the Club came of age the civilian tail would have wagged the military dog – had it not been for the veto exercised by the President.

The imbalance became so great and the intransigence of the Commanding Officer so blinkered that there was only one way out. The civilians must set up their own Club. They did and the story might be left here, were it not that the process by which civilians and volunteers became independent illustrates how a nineteenth century Club conducted its business, admittedly in unusual circumstances. The Minutes of the interminable succession of interminable meetings leading to the schism would fill a small volume. The reader must be content with edited highlights.

Curiously enough the increase in the number of civilian members put them at a temporary disadvantage. The original Club Room in Mrs Doggett's Cottage by the Windmill was no longer big enough, so in 1871 the Club became tenants of the London Scottish Iron House, a large corrugated iron building at the Roehampton end of the Common which the Corps used as local headquarters. The civilians were thus more beholden to the Corps. A concession was made to democracy in 1873 when civilians were allowed to provide a third of the Committee; and six years later the Corps agreed that the Captain (hitherto always a Corps member) should be chosen from the whole Club. But the President's veto, a Damocles sword, still hung over the civilians.

The parting of the ways became inevitable when, in November 1878, the Secretary, Henry Lamb, proposed the removal of the limit on civilian Committee Members, pointing out that 250 of the Club's 300 Members were civilians entitled to pro rata representation. Guy Pym thought Lamb had gone too far, and suggested equal membership, which was agreed at a General Meeting. The Chairman, Captain Collyer (a member of the Corps), submitted the resolution to the President, now Lieutenant Colonel Henry Lumsden (taking his orders from Elcho) who immediately vetoed it. Lamb now sent all Club Members a copy of the resolution, explaining it had been vetoed, and urging them to attend an Extraordinary General Meeting, at which it became apparent that the Corps were mainly worried by the danger that the new Clubhouse then being sought would be too far from their Iron House headquarters.

On 14 March 1879 Lumsden told the Captain (Colonel George Moncrieff) that the Corps agreed to a fifty-fifty Committee, and the election of the Captain from the whole membership. But the 'regimental constitution of the Club' was unchanged, and the veto must remain. These points were debated at the Spring Meeting, presided over by Lumsden. Corps members wanted the status quo. Civilians wanted the veto removed. Lumsden refused to agree that it should be used only in matters affecting the Corps. On 19 June 1879 he wrote to Lamb from his Aberdeenshire stronghold, Pitcaple Castle, saying that as the fifty-fifty proposal had not been formally ratified, the one-third rule was deemed to be still in force. When he took the chair at the Autumn Meeting at Mellon's Hotel, Covent Garden (with Elcho present), he confirmed this, and the meeting – little more than a slanging match – broke up in disorder.

On 23 December Lumsden sent a circular rallying all Members to the cause of the Corps. Henry Lamb countered by expressing surprise that he had not told the Committee what he was up to. He was using his position as Commanding Officer to force through a proposition he had failed to get accepted as President. He had a duty to the Club as well as to the Corps. The next General Meeting was held on 22 April 1880, but Lumsden did not attend. The Corps was defended by Captain Collyer, well disposed to the civilians. He tried to heal the breach by proposing that the Commanding Officer should exercise his veto only if the rights of the Corps were adversely affected. If this were agreed the Corps would see it as an olive branch. The civilians gladly fell in with this proposal.

Lumsden was not interested in an olive branch. He fired his next shot on 27 May 1880, when he wrote to Lamb:

> Dear Sir,
>
> With reference to the letter I addressed to you on 23rd Decr. last I regret to say that, finding the opposition of a certain section of the members of the London Scottish Golf Club to its original constitution, and to the power thereby vested in the CO of the Regt. of preventing the adoption of any rule which in his opinion may interfere with the interests of the Corps in any way, still continues, I have no choice but to give notice to the Committee in accordance with the conditions of their lease of the room at the Iron House of the termination of their tenancy at the end of 6 months from 1st June next, which I have done officially to the Secretary.
>
> This disagreeable alternative is forced on me by the action of a portion of the Executive of the Club and some of its members, who wish to set aside the conditions under which the room was let to the Club ...
>
> The past history of the Club, and the fact that as Golfers the interests of the Corps and non-Corps members are identical should be sufficient to assure you that the power thus retained in the hands of the CO will never be exercised in any way to interfere with your enjoyment of the game on Wimbledon Common to the full extent and on thoroughly golfing principles.
>
> To my last letter above referred to, I received many favourable, and only 11 unfavourable replies, notwithstanding a circular issued to you by the Secretary requesting you not to answer mine. As he may probably adopt a similar course again I have now to state that the accommodation in the Iron House will only be available to such members of the Club as agree to use it on the conditions of the present lease, and if you wish to use the Room under these terms I request you will sign and return to me the enclosed paper with as little delay as possible.
>
> I remain
> Yours truly
> Henry Lumsden
> Lt. Col. LSRV and President LS Golf Club

Lumsden enclosed a form to be returned (a copy, complete with unused halfpenny stamp, survives) confirming that the Commanding Officer should be President and that the Presidential veto should continue. Lamb was ready with his rejoinder. He wrote to Lumsden on 2 June with the backing of the whole Committee regretting that he had again communicated direct with Members. The Committee believed they had the support of the great majority. Far from opposing the Commanding Officer's veto, the last General Meeting had agreed to give him full jurisdiction over everything affecting the rights of Corps members.

Yet another Special Meeting was held in July 1880 to consider the notice to quit the Iron House, which would leave the Club homeless on 1 December. When the Committee announced they had found a replacement at the Wimbledon end of the Common they were congratulated and authorized to negotiate a lease. (See Chapter 10: *Clubhouses.*) Although the Meeting was concerned only with the new Clubhouse the question of the veto came up. Mr David Laing, a dedicated Corps member, asked if the Commanding Officer had approved the new Clubhouse as required by the constitution? Moncrieff replied that since Lumsden had thrown them out of the Iron House 'he could not for one moment suppose they had any reason to ask him anything about the matter. (Hear! Hear! and applause)'. Laing persisted after being rulled out of order. They were bound to get the Commanding Officer's approval. He shut up only when asked if he was there as the agent of Lumsden, who once again had failed to appear.

For all practical purposes the battle was over, although the debate continued at the Autumn Meeting. This was the longest in the history of the Club, and may merit a place in the *Guinness Book of Records*. It began at Mellon's Hotel, Covent Garden on 11 November 1880, was adjourned to St James' Hall Restaurant on 13 December 1880, and further adjourned to the Criterion on 3 February 1881. Colonel Moncrieff brilliantly carried his bat through all three sessions.

Lord Elcho, who said Colonel Lumsden (unavoidably absent) had invested him with power to act for the Regiment, proposed a Committee to 'consider the present position of the London Scottish Golf Club'. That is, to pick up the pieces. After hours of discussion in which the civilians made it clear that they were perfectly content to leave things as they were, the meeting agreed to Elcho's committee. By 13 December when the meeting reconvened, the Corps had shown an astonishing new interest in golf. The Chairman did not want to make capital out of this manoeuvre but others did. The Secretary, when asked about Members who had joined since 11 November, began to read the list with obvious relish, but was told just to give the number. The answer – 29 new Members, 13 having joined that very day, and all having paid their subscriptions – was greeted with laughter and hisses. A former member of the Corps, Mr J. S. Anderson, said he would oppose the break-up of the Club, if only the introduction of faggot voters was banned. When Elcho asked him what he meant, he replied 'I used the term "faggot votes" as a short term for the manufacture of votes for an express purpose. (Hear, hear, and laughter.)'. Someone else referred to a rumour that a member of the Corps had offered £20 to bring in 40 men to vote. Without attempting to explain the sudden popularity of golf in the Corps among men who had never wielded a club in anger, Elcho said they had every right to join. 'Many of them – all of them, I hope – will turn out good Golfers. (Laughter.) I suppose you all began some time or other. (Hear, hear, and laughter.) Some as children; some as middle-aged; and some, I am happy to say, for the pleasure of Golf as old men; and therefore I repeat that I hope these "faggots" will be good and efficient Golfers.'

The purpose of the meeting was to consider the report of the Committee set up in November. It recommended that the CO should continue as President, the Captain would be elected from the whole Club, the Committee would be fifty-fifty. If the Secretary was a civilian, the Treasurer must be from the Corps and vice versa; and any threat to the interests of the Corps would be referred to the President. Two of the three non-Corps Members on the Committee, including Moncrieff, went along with the report. The third, Guy Pym, said it increased the power of the CO, and refused to sign. The meeting – by 82 votes to 80 – agreed to refer the matter back to the Special Committee. Before they broke up – far into the night – Moncrieff, fearing that the 1880 Autumn General Meeting might still be going strong in the Autumn of 1881, issued a word of warning. If the Committee could not reach an amicable settlement, they must at once legislate for an amicable separation.

The final report of the Special Committee, submitted to the adjourned General Meeting on 3 February, was short and to the point. A scheme for reconstituting the Club with unanimous support was beyond reach. Those Corps members who had resolved to leave the Club (and no doubt the faggots) should have their 1881 subscriptions refunded and take with them certain trophies. If they formed a new Club, there should be a Joint Committee to maintain the Course and arrange play.

It might be thought that all Members would thankfully accept the position; but no. Mr Laing had a last fling in a bitter and slanderous speech. The Corps members were the Club, and the non-Corps members the people who had been admitted ... On the supposition that they were gentlemen, the non-Corps members were allowed on the Committee, first of all one-third to two-thirds, and afterwards half and half; but the Committee as at present constituted, instead of representing them, misrepresented them ... Mr Lamb had become Secretary to gain his own ends. (Loud cries of 'Order'.) He would repeat that the Secretary had used his position to further his objective, namely to turn the members of the Volunteer Corps out of their own Club. ('No! No!'.) The Colonel of the Corps was in the same position as the proprietor of a proprietary club, and retained certain rights. If he chose to enforce his legal veto, they would all be turned out. If they chose to act in the manner they proposed, he could hardly call it the conduct of gentlemen. Not only were they taking funds which did not belong to them, but they were also going to take away the medals.

This hysterical outburst was the only discordant note as the marathon General Meeting drew to a close and accepted the Special Committee's

The London Scottish Rifle Volunteers 'Iron House' on Wimbledon Common near Roehampton, the first Clubhouse.

formula for peaceful separation and friendly coexistence. That no bitterness remained is witnessed by the fact that Elcho (proposed by A. J. Balfour) and Lumsden were later elected Members of Royal Wimbledon.

Two Clubs had now evolved from the original; but they retained the same name, or almost. The civilians claimed 'The London Scottish Golf Club', perhaps to emphasize that it was the Corps that had seceded. The Corps put inverted commas round 'London Scottish' in their own name, which amused the civilians. Six months later the civilians still claimed the original name, and Henry Lamb wrote to *The Field* complaining about their reference to 'The Wimbledon Golf Club'. There was no such Club. A few men had started a new Club at the Iron Shooting House, and had all but appropriated 'our name, the only distinction being the inverted commas'. An anonymous correspondent, claiming membership of both Clubs, suggested that 'the confusion might be fitly terminated, perhaps by the Wimbledon players gracefully declining a title which no longer expresses their nationality or constitution, and their retention of which serves only to irritate their former friends . . .'.

It was not until April 1882 that the Club acted on this advice. Moncrieff, writing in the name of the London Scottish, humbly requested that the Prince of Wales (later Edward VII) should continue as Patron of the Club after they changed their name to 'The Wimbledon Golf Club'; and that he should agree to their using the prefix 'Royal'. His Royal Highness gladly consented to be Patron, but it was not in his power to make the Club 'Royal'. That was for the Home Office. Henry Lamb duly applied to that Department, and on 6 June 1882 was informed that Her Majesty was graciously pleased to accede to the Club's request, and to command that the Wimbledon Golf Club shall be styled Royal Wimbledon Golf Club.

Edward Scudamore in his account of the events chronicled above describes the principal actors as he saw them:

> The picture of our forebears which emerges is of a virile and turbulent race who hurled monstrous accusations at each other with an abandon which would hardly find acceptance today. I have developed a profound regard for that courteous and polished gentleman, Colonel Moncrieff. I would dearly love to spend a little time at the bar with that charming young scapegrace, Captain Collyer. I stand a little in awe of the cool and calculating Henry Lamb ... For the sake of peace and harmony I would hastily agree with any views expressed by Mr Guy Pym, while if Lord Elcho entered the Clubhouse I should deem it wise to stand to attention.

Of Elcho it can be said there was no doubt about his dedication to golf. In 1880 he took the Professional Tom Dunn to Felixstowe (where he often visited Orwell Park for the partridge shooting) to spy out the land for a golf course. It is recorded in the History of the Felixstowe Golf Club:

> Tom Dunn's favourable report on the character of the ground, and the enthusiasm of Lord Elcho, soon spread to the Wimbledon Club, and at Whitsuntide the brothers Frank and Alexander Crawford went down to Bawdsey Ferry and enjoyed a game over the close-cropped turf. They were followed on the August Bank Holiday by a party from the London Scottish Golf Club. They cut nine holes and played for a Challenge Medal ... Thus the 'Bawdsey Challenge Gold Medal' became the first of the Club's valuable trophies, although it was originally referred to as the Wimbledon Gold Medal as the donors were all Members of that Club.

Elcho, Felixstowe's first President, started golf at the age of 14, and was still playing at 92. 'When he became weary of walking between shots, he rode sedately on a chestnut cob which always accompanied him in his later years.' He died at the age of 96.

Three

IMAGES

O wad some Pow'r the giftie gie us
To see oorsels as ithers see us,
It wad frae mony a blunder free us.

ROBERT BURNS, untutored in the simple pleasures of gowff (though he would have been a low handicap man at the Nineteenth), hit the nail on the head in the context of the Royal and Ancient Game. Nothing mystifies the non-golfer more than the weekly pilgrimage from first to eighteenth. To the golfer nothing is more divinely right. Were he aware of the image he presents to the rest of mankind, were he to freeze at the top of the back swing and ask himself just why he is in this curious position – that way madness lies.

That golf in England was still a considerable mystery in the 1860s is revealed by an article in *The Graphic* in 1869 which informed its readers that

> For golf the first, indispensable requirement is a large open tract of common (in Scotland termed a 'link') in which are sunk a series of holes, four inches in diameter, at distances of from one to three or four hundred yards apart. The rival sides, each provided with a set of clubs and balls endeavour, in the fewest number of strokes, to place the balls in the series of holes.

It is not surprising that the exponents of a new game, played in a public place, and arguably dangerous to third parties, should have been unpopular with their fellow citizens. In the earliest days there was no doubt in the minds of many residents of Wimbledon and Putney, in particular those liable for the Common rate, that golfers were a menace to society. Nobly led by Mr Flemmich of Alton House, Roehampton, they campaigned against the golfers, saddling the Conservators with the impossible task of ensuring justice for both sides. In June 1873 Flemmich headed a group opposed to golf on the Common. The Conservators appointed a committee of ratepayers and golfers 'to arrange terms and regulations which may be satisfactory to both parties as to time, space, and mode of playing the Game'. A vain hope. Solomon himself could not have handed down an acceptable judgement. Many ratepayers wanted no golf. Many golfers wanted to play every day.

A year later Flemmich was still carrying the banner of the citizens of Roehampton, claiming that the golfers were denying their children the use of the Common. He had consulted his neighbours, who believed that unless players kept strictly to the Wimbledon end of the Common, there was no spot where they did not interfere with the comfort and safety of the residents of Roehampton. This public spirit, not dissimilar to that of latter-day peace-loving Stansted, simply meant that Roehampton would be content if the golfing menace were transferred to Wimbledon. Flemmich went further:

> ... I only express the general opinion of my neighbours and myself in saying that the Game of Golf is one which cannot be allowed on Wimbledon Common, except by infringing the rights and privileges of those who use the Common for quiet recreation and exercise; and I feel convinced that the Conservators will best consider the general feeling of the residents by prohibiting the game altogether.

The Conservators put off the evil day by a decision to study the whole question of games on the Common; but in February 1875 they gave way to pressure from their Roehampton constituents by proposing that the Golf Course should start at the Windmill and not at the London Scottish Iron House near Roehampton. Further, there should be no extension of the golf season, which ran from September to May. The golfers agreed to abandon play in the neighbourhood of the Iron House, provided they could have a cottage near the Windmill as a Clubhouse, to which the Conservators agreed.

In 1878 the Conservators sought Counsel's opinion about the use of the Common for golf, and were rewarded with advice which left them on a more delicate tightrope than ever:

> As to the game of golf I am of opinion that the Conservators cannot prohibit it, but they are not bound to give any facilities for it. They may prescribe a particular part of the Common for this pastime if they choose, and I do not think such a regulation would be open to objection as being an appropriation to a particular Club of part of the Common. Anybody may come on the Common and play golf, and the London Scottish have no exclusive right to use the holes they have made. The players are liable to actions if they hurt anyone, and to be prosecuted for manslaughter if anyone is killed, but I do not think they commit any breach of the bye-laws in making the holes or smoothing the turf round. If they did, I think the bye-laws would be bad, for the right to play a game implies the right to do all that is necessary to play it.

This maintained the status quo. The Golf Club for its part reminded Members of the need to keep a low profile and to avoid providing ammunition to their opponents. They were 'earnestly requested to be particularly careful not to play balls near people walking or riding on the Common, and also not to address any person crossing the Common in a manner calculated to give offence'. In 1880, however, the ratepayers, alarmed by the increase in the numbers playing golf, became more militant. The Club sought to spike their guns by suspending the election of new Members, except that ratepayers and their sons over 18 would still be accepted because 'it was deemed so important to conciliate the people of the neighbourhood'. They assured the Conservators that everything was being done to make Members behave properly. Nevertheless, the anti-golf lobby went ahead with a 'memorial' signed by 92 ratepayers, including the indefatigable Mr Flemmich.

They objected to the great interference with the proper use of the Common caused by the game of golf which

> requires a very extensive area of ground, the balls are struck with great violence and driven to a considerable distance, and the gound or course being occupied by a constant succession of players (frequently more than 100) the result is that practically the whole length of the Course, which is upward of a mile, is monopolised for this game, and the public entirely excluded from using it.

Exercise and recreation were rendered impossible. The Common could not be traversed with safety while the game of golf was played, which it was on every day except Sundays from early morning to late in the evening. Because of the risk of being struck by the balls, ladies, nursemaids and children were afraid to go near the ground. A very objectionable accompaniment of the game was the assemblage of idle rough boys hanging about waiting to carry the sticks of the players or pick up their lost balls. The fact that Wimbledon was so near the Metropolis meant that much of the Common was taken over by a few people, mostly non-residents, at the expense of locals who paid for the amenity.

Another memorial signed by 66 ratepayers accepted that golf on the Common had come to stay, and suggested that only residents should play. Three days a week would be quite enough; and there should be no golf on Saturday when many people visited the Common. The sponsors of this memorial put the Conservators on the spot by arguing that the occupation, not to say the monopoly, of a large area of the Common by a private Club of gentlemen mostly resident in London was not something they could reasonably countenance.

The gentleman who submitted this memorial admitted that his business engagements allowed him to enjoy the Common only on Sunday and he had not personally suffered at the hands of the golfers; but he was satisfied that they had no exclusive right over any part of the Common. It was for them to give way to passers-by and not, as usually happened, for the golfers to tell the passers-by to give way to them.

On 30 May 1881 a meeting was attended at the Conservators' office in Lincoln's Inn Fields by all the interested parties – Lord Elcho and Colonel Lumsden from 'the Iron House Golf Club', Henry Lamb and Colonel Moncrieff from 'the Golf Club at Croft's premises' (the descriptions used by the Conservators' Minute writer), and Sir Edward Pearson and Mr Murray for the ratepayers. Murray read a letter in favour of continuing golf under proper regulations. The Clerk read the memorials against the game. The 'Iron House Golf Club' submitted they had done everything in their power to make the game safe. They had restricted membership to 150. They had changed their Club days from Wednesday and Saturday to Thursday and Saturday. They had asked Members not to use the Course on Bank and Public holidays, and not to hit 'while any person is within range, or where the ball might fall' – implying perhaps that no Member of the Club ever shanked.

Henry Lamb offered further concessions. Friday was the day of least value, but there was no objection to giving up Wednesdays. The game might be allowed in the morning on days other than Club days (showing that golf was played every day except Sunday). Two holes near Stag (or Sixpenny) Lane, which were thought to be particularly dangerous, could be modified; and a plan setting out proposed alterations would be submitted to the Conservators.

Having heard all the arguments, the Conservators drew up regulations which they hoped the ratepayers would regard as adequate. They set apart for the playing of the game of golf parts of the Common ('hereinafter called tees') containing 240 square feet, and other parts ('hereinafter called golf lawns') being circular in form and 75 feet in diameter

> provided always that no part of the said tees or golf lawns shall be inclosed nor shall any person be prevented from walking or riding thereon: and provided that no other part of the Common than the said tees and golf lawns, and the spaces intervening in a straight line (as near as may be) between the said tees and golf lawns respectively shall be used for the playing of the game of golf.

Thus hooking and slicing, as well as shanking, were now prohibited by law. The Conservators were more generous about Club days than the ratepayers hoped, approving Tuesday, Thursday and Saturday between sunrise and sunset; but golf was to be played at no other time. Further no-one might strike a ball 'near any person walking, riding, or driving [a carriage, not a golf ball] over the Common, or otherwise play at golf in such a manner as to injure, endanger, alarm or annoy any person traversing or being on the Common for exercise, recreation, or other lawful purpose; or require any person crossing the Common between any tee and any golf lawn to move away, or otherwise interfere with any such person'.

For some years there was an uneasy truce in which the golfers did their best to stick to the regulations. Royal Wimbledon reminded Members that 'the ordinary warning of "Fore!" is not deemed sufficient at Wimbledon'. The Head Common Keeper was instructed to report to the Conservators the names and addresses of people playing on the forbidden days, who were occasionally threatened with prosecution, but never actually taken to court. When someone complained about the recklessness of a golfer, the Conservators told him they had no power to prosecute, but had sent his complaint on to the Golf Club. On the other hand when Mr Flemmich reported 'an instance of a golf ball falling between himself and a friend and hitting their dog' he was told that the Conservators would prosecute if they were furnished with the name of the offender and independent witnesses. The handful of complaints received year by year were similarly dealt with, and the ratepayers seem to have accepted there was little more they could do.

At least in one case a Member of Royal Wimbledon protested about dangerous play. It is recorded in a breathless Minute that Mr Godden, living at 4 Camp View, complained

> of the intolerable inconvenience caused by the reckless play of some golfers on the Common, that golf balls had twice within the last twelve months been sent under a carriage in which Mrs Godden was driving, and on several occasions Mrs Godden and other ladies had been nearly struck by balls when walking, and that the Common was becoming dangerous for children, that on several occasions balls had been sent into his garden or had hit his fence, and that on the 12th of April the scullery window was broken, and that splinters of glass had been sent all over the floor, that he was afraid that unless some steps were taken to enable people to walk on the Common in safety, he should be obliged to resign his membership, in order that he might have a free hand to take such steps as might be available for stopping the nuisance.

This is a unique instance of a golfer seeing himself 'as ithers saw him'. We may be forgiven if we suggest that 'the Pow'r' that made this possible was Mr Godden's wife. He wrote not as a golfer, but under orders from the aggrieved Mrs Godden. The Club came to his rescue by declaring the area in the immediate neighbourhood of 4 Camp Road out of bounds – surely only partial relief, since there is no law – judicial or natural – that can keep a ball within bounds, and without neighbouring sculleries.

A precautionary measure, first advocated by Royal Wimbledon, was instituted in 1892 – the wearing of red coats, which Common golfers have been required to do ever since. Worried by the successful prosecution of a certain Mr Lockhart 'for driving a ball to the alarm of a passer-by', the Club urged Members to wear red. The Conservators' bye-law was specific: 'No male person shall play golf on the Men's Course after 10 am without wearing a red coat or some other exterior garment coloured red'. Inevitably someone tried to get round it. Mr C. B. Marsham was reported by a fellow Member for playing 'without a red coat, but with a red hat'. Mr Marsham was informed 'that his contention that a red hat fulfilled the regulation' was neither within the spirit nor the wording of the bye-law.

The Conservators sent questionnaires to 2183 ratepayers asking if they approved the extension of golf playing to every day except Sunday between 1 November and 31 March.

The extension was supported by 437 ratepayers; and opposed by 801. 20 failed to make their views clear; and 125 didn't mind either way. The majority verdict was accepted.

This suspended the triangular contest – Conservators v. golfers v. ratepayers. Its resumption is described in the next chapter.

Four

CONSERVATORS

WHEN THE CONSERVATORS took over the Common in 1871, golf there was an accomplished fact. They found themselves holding a balance between Golf Club Members, casual golfers who could not be denied the use of the Course, and the general public frequenting the Common for exercise and recreation.

By 1879 overcrowding of the Course had become a serious problem. The number of Club Members was limited by agreement with the Conservators, but the growing popularity of the game brought increasing numbers of casual golfers to the Links, to the discomfort of the Clubs. They suggested easing the congestion by allowing play on five rather than three days a week in return for which they would admit all ratepayers on the waiting list. They also asked that no new Club should play on the Common until a second Course was laid out; and that something should be done to discourage casual golfers. The Conservators could not see their way to act on these requests.

Overcrowding got steadily worse, and in 1905 Royal Wimbledon and London Scottish made a joint approach to the Conservators. They complained that the many newcomers did not understand golf, were a danger to the public, and on competition days were a great nuisance. If they caused a serious accident the Clubs would be blamed. They had spent a great deal on the Course and the restriction on membership meant that a limited number of Members were providing free golf for an ever-increasing number of casual players.

They proposed 'in a friendly spirit and without going into legal considerations or alleged rights either of the Golf Clubs or the public' that Keepers should be employed to enforce the regulations; and that casual golfers be given starting times by the Conservators, to whom they should pay a green fee for the benefit of the Clubs. The Conservators now agreed that something must be done. They proposed that casual golfers should register, and pay a green fee of 2s.6d. a round. Would the Clubs keep the registers, engage someone to issue tickets, and collect the green fees? Royal Wimbledon agreed, except that the

Caddy Master, rather than a specially appointed official, would issue tickets. The London Scottish followed suit. In the event these arrangements did not work, as in the absence of statutory backing few troubled to pay a green fee.

There was a threat of even greater congestion in 1907 when the Wimbledon Town Club applied to play on the Common. At first their application (supported by Royal Wimbledon) was turned down, but a year later the Conservators agreed they should use the Common Course with the same rights as the other Clubs. At the same time they took a census to find out just how many casual players were using the Course. It was revealed that on seven days in December 1908 when golf was allowed interlopers accounted for 126 rounds – more than 10% of the 1,149 played. (Royal Wimbledon Members played 460, London Scottish, 284, and Wimbledon Town, 279.) The number enjoying free golf was high enough to persuade the Conservators to make a change. Their solution was to impose a charge on all players – Club Members and non-members alike – the proceeds to be devoted to the maintenance of the Course. The Office of Works, responsible for the activities of the Board of Conservators, saw no difficulty in the proposals.

Royal Wimbledon decided to oppose them, and asked for the support of the other Clubs. The Mayor of Wimbledon, Cecil Walsh, wrote to the First Commissioner of Works (Lewis Harcourt MP) as 'landlord of a small piece of shooting which you rent from me at Stanton Court', asking him to hold his hand. This made the First Commissioner pause. He thought he had already approved the new bye-laws but told the Mayor he would consider representations. Walsh replied that the Conservators were not unanimous. Some wanted the bye-laws ratified *sub silentio* 'at the instance of the London Scottish Golf Club, which is a declining body, with some end of its own apparently in view. The Royal Wimbledon, which numbers 550 and has a really influential and increasing membership is opposed to the bye-laws, and also the Town Club recently formed, a successful body of tradesmen and others who cannot afford the subscriptions of the other Clubs'.

Petitions were duly submitted by Royal Wimbledon, London Scottish, Wimbledon Town, and Wimbledon Ladies' Clubs. These splendid documents, beautifully engrossed, survive in the nation's archives at Kew, testimony to the importance of golf in the life of the community: 'In the Matter of the Wimbledon and Putney Commons Act, 1871: Bye laws with respect to Golf: To the Right Honourable the First Commissioner of His Majesty's Works and Public Buildings: The humble Petition of The Royal Wimbledon Golf Club of Camp Cottage Wimbledon in the County of Surrey acting through the Committee of the said Club, Sheweth' and so on for four copperplate pages, concluding with the traditional undertaking (unlikely to be implemented) 'That your Petitioners will ever pray etc etc'.

Royal Wimbledon claimed that the Conservators had no power to make all pay a green fee, but they should levy a charge on non-members. The London Scottish accepted they could impose a charge on all, but also hoped it would be collected only from non-members. The Town Club (now with 205

Members out of a permitted 250) echoed Royal Wimbledon's belief that the Clubs must be exempt from any charges. Further, they feared that when it was known that anyone could play on payment of a green fee 'the Links will be flooded with persons desirous of doing so, and golf will then be rendered almost impossible'. The Ladies' petition, appropriately signed by their Secretary, Gertrude Tee, followed Royal Wimbledon's, adding that their nine-hole Course had 'added materially to the general prosperity of Wimbledon and Putney, and increased the amenity of the neighbourhood both to local residents and to visitors'.

The Official Solicitor, when called on to brief the First Commissioner, had no difficulty in demolishing the mass of argument presented by the Clubs. The suggestion that the bye-laws would limit the use of the Common 'for purposes of exercise and recreation' was nonsense. The golfers were simply hoping to continue to profit by people's ignorance of their rights. In citing Section 84 of the Act in support of their contention that the Clubs could not be required to pay green fees they were on weak ground. That Section also dealt with nuisances. 'The swift propulsion of a hard ball through the air ... is probably a nuisance, at least if not properly regulated [by statute rather than by the player] ... By the non-golf-playing inhabitants the golfers are looked on as a dangerous nuisance.' Some objections cancelled each other out. The fear that golf would be restricted by the imposition of a charge did not square with the Town Club's claim that the Common would be flooded with golfers.

When the First Commissioner, armed with this nine-page brief, faced the petitioners and a deputation from the Council on 25 May 1909, he must have felt on secure ground. He made a point of asking if the Conservators were unanimous; and was assured they were. Could he go and play tomorrow if he wanted to? Yes. Provided he had a red coat and a caddy. There would be no green fee.

The Commissioners' Clerk batted first. He pointed out that the bye-laws would overcome difficulties caused by the popularity of golf. The charge was to be for the use of the green, not for playing [a nice distinction]. Nowhere in Britain could one play without contributing to the upkeep of the Course. St Andrews' ratepayers might seem to play free but in fact they paid through the rates, since The Royal and Ancient operated under an Act of Parliament making the municipality responsible for the Course. There were many precedents for charging green fees, for example at Bournemouth and Epping Forest. The Conservators believed that Club Members must pay like everyone else; but their green fees, supplemented by those from the public, would be used to maintain the Course. He could not understand the Clubs' objections. They would not be a penny worse off. Indeed, they would be better off. The Wimbledon Council's objection was equally incomprehensible. The bye-laws did not make the Course one whit more public that it already was.

A. G. Rickards KC, Captain of Royal Wimbledon, claimed that no case had been made out for major change. The Town Club concurred. Norman Foster, on behalf of the Ladies, said they wanted to be left alone. Considering how few played, it would be a ridiculous waste of money to make them employ an official to collect green fees. Only the London Scottish were impressed by the Conservators' case. They now agreed they had found the best solution. In summing up, the First Commissioner said his task was to protect not golfers, but the public, two important sections of which had not been represented – golfers not members of the Clubs, and non-golfers who thought the game a dangerous nuisance. He did not expect the deputations to share that view but they knew quite well there were those who, when their children were hit by golf balls, had strong feelings about the game.

It seems likely that the Clerk and the London Scottish representatives left the hearing confident they had won. It must have come as a great shock to the former when he received a private letter from the First Commissioner saying he was not prepared to confirm the bye-laws, and suggesting they should be withdrawn to allow the matter to lapse. The Conservators, justly incensed, demanded an explanation 'so as to place the responsibility upon him of refusing to confirm the bye-laws which in the opinion of the regulating authority were necessary'. The First Commissioner did not deign to reply to this questioning of his authority. The Departmental Secretary said his master did not feel bound to state his reasons. 'His action was taken upon a general consideration of all the circumstances which had been laid before him.'

That was the end of the matter until 1913 when the London Scottish and Wimbledon Town Club approached the Conservators once again about the better regulation of the game. The Conservators found themselves in difficulty because they had no idea why their earlier application had been refused. They guessed it was due to the opposition of some Members of Royal Wimbledon and London Scottish who had been afraid that the bye-laws would encourage large numbers to use the Course. It is difficult to understand why Royal Wimbledon did oppose the bye-laws. They had their own new Course; and would have been better off financially had they agreed to the Conservators' plans.

An equally great mystery is why the First Commissioner failed to support the Conservators, who had done everything possible to ensure justice in a situation where perfect justice was unattainable. The Mayor of Wimbledon may have undermined him by his hint that the Conservators were divided. A parliamentary question may have had some effect. Would the First Commissioner before approving the new bye-laws 'insist on proper precautions to protect the public from injury by golf balls?'. A serious accident after he had blessed the legislation would not be a vote catcher.

Another possibility, to be dismissed out of hand, is that the First Commissioner got it into his head that if he made a wrong decision his shooting rights might be prejudiced.

Five

COURSES

FOR THE FIRST SIX YEARS the Course on the Common was limited to seven holes encircling the Windmill, three rounds being played to approximate to the standard eighteen. Early in 1871 the Club, uncertain about the attitude which the Board of Conservators would adopt towards a game which many of the general public thought required a disproportionate amount of space, believed that if the Course was to be extended, it was now or never. Tom Dunn, the Professional, was instructed 'to pick out some new holes' enlarging the Course to eighteen. According to his later account, quoted in an American newspaper, an influential Committee member who had just learned there were eighteen holes at St Andrews, took him aside and 'whispered in a hoarse voice: "Tom, let us have one more". "Och, that is impossible", I replied. "Eighteen is the orthodox number"'. The other insisted, and Dunn reluctantly gave way. When he told the Committee he had laid out nineteen holes 'Well, you never in your life saw a more excited lot of men. There was an uproar and all made a dive for poor Mr Grant. The fellow never heard the last of it, and to the day of his death was known as "Nineteen Hole Grant"'.

The camera cannot capture the whole magic of a golf course. We do better with glimpses through the eyes of contemporaries. Shortly after the Course was completed *The Field* correspondent wrote 'These Links are capable of great improvement. The course [ie fairway] of the third hole is much cut up with heavy carts and horses' hoofs, and off the course are nasty gorse bushes, also long grass and gorse at other holes. The new Clubhouse is nearly finished, and the Links as a whole are not to be despised'. The extended Course was the subject of a more flattering article in *The Field* by Niblick:

> The Wimbledon Links. The Golfing Ground of the London Scottish Golf Club on Wimbledon Common has, thanks to the skill of their Professional, Dunn, been lately so improved and extended as to make it one of the finest Courses in this country ... Within six miles from Hyde Park Corner there is a golfing Links equal in extent, and superior in number and variety of hazards, to the far-famed Links of St Andrews...

> Starting from the new and commodious golf house, the First hole is within a long drive and a quarter stroke, on a fine piece of turf, sloping gently towards a deep ravine. It offers no particular hazards.
>
> The Second hole is reached by a long drive across this ravine which goes by the name of Glen Albin, and is thickly overgrown with whins and shrubs, where many balls lie buried. The hole is situated in a hollow, covered with fine sward.
>
> The Third hole is on the west side of the Windmill enclosure and has a dangerous hazard of whins on its right.
>
> The Fourth hole is within two easy drives, and has a fine hazard of whins all around it.
>
> The Fifth hole is within a long drive, and has a good whin hazard near the starting point.
>
> The Sixth hole is between two rifle butts, and across a dangerous but fortunately not very wide ravine beset with whins and briars, and having a small stream at its bottom.
>
> The Seventh hole is behind the Butts on a smooth piece of turf, surrounded by whins.
>
> The Eighth hole is in front of the last rifle Butt, and is approached by a long and narrow stretch of fine turf, on either side of which is a dense growth of whins; it may be reached by a lofting stroke over the second last Butt, or by the passage between the second and third Butt.
>
> The Ninth hole leads across a wide gravel pit needing a full drive to get over it.
>
> The Tenth hole has no hazards beyond the road, which has to be crossed. The turf here is almost equal to a St Andrews putting green.
>
> The Eleventh hole is not far from the Roman Camp, and is approached through some scattered whins.
>
> The Twelfth hole leads back to the south side of the large gravel pit, and the whins that conceal it may be avoided by keeping well to the right.
>
> The Thirteenth hole is across the gravel pit, the centre of which is studded with tufts of rushes.
>
> The Fourteenth hole is within a cleek stroke in front of the third Butt.
>
> The Fifteenth hole leads through very rough grass, and the course is intersected by a small but rugged ravine which may be avoided by keeping well to the right. Some players prefer the shorter but more perilous course to the left of this ravine.
>
> The Sixteenth hole is by the side of the Windmill garden and has few and inconsiderable hazards.
>
> The Seventeenth hole is on the site of the Victoria Camp and has on the one hand the hazard of the garden, and on the other that of the curling pond, in both of which many balls come to grief.
>
> The Eighteenth and last hole is on the smooth croquet ground adjoining the golf house; and has to be approached across the wide and deep Glen Albin. There is also a good whin hazard surrounding the putting green.
>
> The whole Course is nearly 4 miles in length, and can be played in an hour and a half. A short round of seven holes may be played by turning off from the Fourth to the Sixteenth hole. This is as nearly as possible the old course round the Windmill …

The monthly medal of April 1871 was played over 'one long round' of 18 holes and 'one short round' of 7 holes, 25 holes in all. A very high wind affected the scoring. Two players were tied on 132 – well over level 5s. There was a play-off over the short Course won by 5 shots. The long and short rounds were still being played next year, but soon after this the Course was seen only as 18 holes.

There is an early description in the first number of *The Golfing Annual* (1887–88) in an account by Horace Hutchinson of a fictitious match. The Wimbledon putting greens are by nature bumpy. The bumps led his ball away from the hole and his opponent's towards it [a natural phenomenon that persists today]. 'There is one hole up a narrow ride between high whins – they call it "the race course", but when you come to drive it it hardly looks broad enough for two shelties abreast ... Wimbledon is a wonderfully wild, breezy, natural place to be so near London, and it must do the metropolitans a power of good to carry back some of that air into the city with them.'

The Conservators kept a tight rein on the golfers. All modifications of the Course had to be approved. There was trouble in 1875 when changes made without reference to the Board were objected to by anti-golf ratepayers. The Club was taken to task, but the variations were ratified, except that a hole across the Butts considered dangerous was not allowed. When in the same year the Conservators investigated games on the Common, the Club submitted a memorandum playing down the modifications called for by golf. 'Eighteen small holes 3 inches in diameter and about 3 inches deep are required for the purposes of the game, and the turf for a small distance round each of them is carefully rolled, mown and swept.' The diameter of the greens authorized by the Conservators was 75 feet, and there was trouble when this was exceeded – presumably because the natural wild character of the Common was being impaired. Although golf was not supposed to be played every day, it was. In 1878 the Club indulged in a mild deception. Flags were put out every weekday 'but big flags as too conspicuous and likely to attract too much notice should be reserved for the Club days' when golf was officially allowed.

There was no further change in layout until 1878, when the Club replaced the first hole with another towards Caesar's Camp. In reply to the Conservators' request for information about the use of the Course, the Club's Secretary, Henry Lamb, explained that, although golf was usually played all the year round, on Wimbledon Common there was little play in the summer months, especially when it was occupied by the Rifle Association. Club Members played 'more or less every weekday, but I would venture to point out that from the play being spread out over the whole week the number of players at any one time is reduced, and this tends to remove the inconveniences that a crowded green causes to them, and might also cause to the general public'.

From this time until Royal Wimbledon, in Bernard Darwin's words, 'deserted the Common and migrated to its private and most attractive Course on the other side of the road', the Conservators usually fell in with the Clubs' wishes, but not invariably. Requests to remove stones, preserve the turf round the holes, and cut grass were granted without argument. Liming of rough grass was allowed under the supervision of the Common staff. A water supply for the putting greens was approved subject to an undertaking to remove the pipes if asked to do so. But the Conservators were quick to remind the golfers that they were in charge. When they became aware 'that a new teeing place was being prepared at the rear of the Queen's Butt' they forbade its use until it had been inspected and approved.

There was a minor crisis in 1882 when Royal Wimbledon suggested the London Scottish should contribute towards the upkeep of the Course. They were told that they (the London Scottish) were 'getting a man up from Scotland' to take complete charge of their nine holes. This was more than Royal Wimbledon had bargained for. Hitherto they had looked after the whole Course, and they refused to surrender responsibility for half. They assured the London Scottish that suggestions for the care of the green would be met 'with courteous and considerate attention'; and if they wanted to provide labour it would be gratefully received. But Royal Wimbledon would continue to look after the whole of the green, as they had done for years past. The London Scottish accepted this – and why not, since they were getting an excellent service for nothing.

By 1890 efforts to improve the Course had met with some success, but it was not yet perfect. An article in *Golf* of November in that year considered that:

> The Chief advantages of the Wimbledon Links are their being within easy reach of London, only about seven or eight miles from Waterloo or Hyde Park. From the former by train you arrive at Wimbledon station in about twenty minutes, from Kensington in about thirty minutes. There is always a good supply of cabs at the station and the fare is 1s. 6d. or for four or five persons 6d. each. It takes about fifteen minutes to reach the Clubhouse. The part of the Common over which you play is high and the air bracing, being interspersed with patches of gorse, a few cottages, undulating ground, and an old picturesque windmill standing in the centre. The turf is not precisely the kind that most golfers appreciate, being gravelly, uneven, with patches of remarkably course tough grass ... Three or four years ago it was no uncommon circumstance to have to use your niblick or lofting iron on the greens; a wooden putter was seldom used. Now, however, the greens are really so good you can almost always take a putter, either wood or iron as you may prefer.

Next year Royal Wimbledon expended much effort in improving the Course still further. They laid down a large quantity of Mitcham turf to make new tees, helped by the demolition of the rifle butts which provided good quality soil. The Professional, Patrick, was authorized to buy up to 250 loads. At times the care lavished on the Course seemed a waste of effort. Although the removal of the Riflemen's Camp and the cessation of cavalry manoeuvres (which had annually cut the Course to pieces) helped considerably, tees and greens were still at the mercy of riders and other users of the Common. Boys keen on cricket found the more level greens made admirable wickets, and the Common Keeper was called in to make them take their stumps elsewhere. The Club received an apology from Mrs Osborne, of the Rounds, Wimbledon on behalf of her brother, Mr E. Ross, a Member of the Club, regretting that his butler had insisted on playing football on the Sixteenth green. It would not happen again. A proposal to sink 'Abyssinian wells' to water the greens was

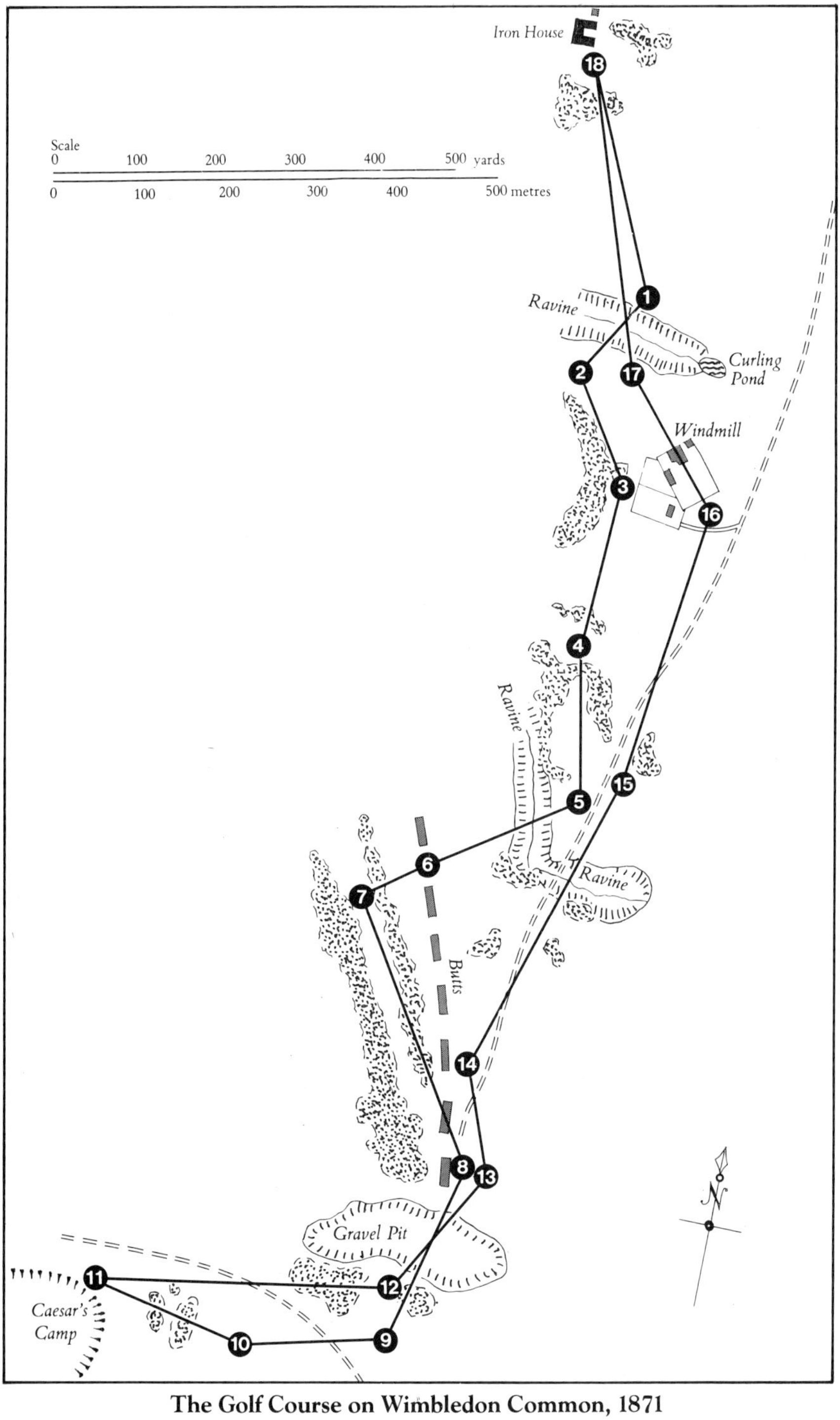

The Golf Course on Wimbledon Common, 1871

not received with enthusiasm by the Conservators. When the Club stockpiled road scrapings for 'dressing the golf green' without permission they were ordered to remove them. Eventually they were allowed to make dumps, provided it was done at times approved by the Head Common Keeper.

In 1899 the two Clubs proposed to move the Course south of a line through Queensmere and the Windmill, but the Conservators thought it would take up too much of the Common. Two years later they offered to extend the Course north towards the now disused Butts, provided the Clubs gave up an area near the Windmill for the use of the public; and in 1901 four new holes were authorized to compensate for those lost at the Windmill. Earth to bottom the new greens might be taken from areas approved by the Ranger, who would also superintend the removal of turf from the abandoned greens; but this must wait until the spring as the Conservators would not countenance bare patches in the winter. Further, they refused to allow sand boxes on tees. It was not until 30 September 1902 that the four new holes were opened. A map of the revised Course was prepared and signed by the Chairman and Clerk of the Conservators, but alas, it has vanished.

In 1907 the Club began to construct their own Course, designed by Willie Park, on 240 acres of Warren Farm adjoining the Common. Charles Ambrose, writing in *The Field*, described the inconvenience of sharing the Common Course:

> Wimbledon Common is open not only to golfers, who play there by courtesy, but also to nursemaids with perambulators, and picnic parties, who find a nicely-kept putting green the very place to spread their tea-things on.

He found the new Course less than perfect:

> Who designed it is not clear. Several people seem to have had a finger in the pie, and when a Course takes shape in that way it is usually altered afterwards.

Bernard Darwin was more charitable. He wrote in *The Golf Courses of Britain* (1910):

> If the Royal Wimbledon golfer dislikes a crowd or a red coat, or if, being a very wicked man or a very busy one, he wishes to play on Sunday, he need nowadays only walk out of the back door of his Clubhouse instead of his front door, and he is on his private course at Caesar's Camp. A wonderful place is this new Wimbledon Course, for as soon as we are on it all signs of men, houses and omnibuses, and the other symptoms of a busy suburb, disappear as if by magic, and a prospect of glorious solitary woods stretches away into the distance in every direction.

It is still the same, seventy-five years later, except that the skyline viewed from the Eighth tee is marred by the high rise monstrosities of Tolworth.

A description of the 1907 layout, related to the present Course, has been provided by Bunny Millard (Captain in 1954–55) who played the 1907 Course for four years from 1920; and is illuminated by Bernard Darwin's description in 1922. It will give those who play the Course today an idea of the route their predecessors followed until 1924.

Millard **FIRST** **Darwin**

266 yards, Bogey 4. Tee by present Flagstaff. Drive to plateau by present Eighteenth tee. Second shot down to two-tier green.

We begin at Wimbledon with rather a curious hole where a really long straight drive will reap a very rich reward. We drive straight at a guide flag with clumps of trees and bushes on either hand ... A well-struck tee shot will send the ball over the brow and down the hill and we may be putting for a two. It is an amusing hole but just a little chancy. However, golf would be dull if we never got more nor less than our just deserts.

SECOND

486 yards, Bogey 5. Walk through wood to Second tee at near (east) end of present Practice Ground. A fine long hole past Warren Cottage along present Fourteenth fairway to present Fourteenth green.

At the Second hole we need entertain no hopes of fortuitous aid. We must do all the work ourselves, by hitting two good wooden shots, and then pitch on to a plateau green with interesting and difficult runs and curves in it.

THIRD

270 yards, Bogey 4. Walk through wood past present Fifth tee to Third tee on present Second fairway. Play to Caesar's Camp through what is now a wood and gorse area left of the top fairway to the present Sixth green.

It is an interesting hole, this Third, with a small mound in front of the green – rather reminiscent of St Andrews. A carefully steered shot gives a run up past the mound, otherwise the situation demands a deft chip.

FOURTH

440 yards, Bogey 5. A fine two-shot hole from the present Seventh tee to a position near the present Seventh green.

The Fourth is a long two-shot hole – very often two and a bit – down a gentle slope with rough country on either side. There is a ridge across the fairway [the rampart of Caesar's Camp] at just the distance that makes a good drive ... the green is well guarded by hummocks and a 5 is always likelier than a 4.

FIFTH

150 yards, Bogey 3. Tee behind and to the right of the present Eighth tee, by the boundary fence. Iron shot (jigger) to a Punch Bowl green 40 yards right and ahead of the present Ladies' Eighth tee.

We should have a 3 at the Fifth, a short hole with a green in a most engaging dell and friendly helpful banks to be reached with a firm iron shot.

SIXTH

260 yards, Bogey 4. Drive from tee below and right of alternative Ladies' Fifth tee, out of the confines of the present Course to a green near Beverley Brook. [This hole and next tee have been taken back by Wimbledon Council.]

We plunge downhill into the low countries to the Sixth hole where a really long shot reaps its reward by giving an easy run up and perhaps a putt for 3; more often, however, it is a rather commonplace 4.

SEVENTH

300 yards, Bogey 5. Drive from the vicinity of Beverley Brook near the footpath, over the present Ninth tee to the present Ninth green. A difficult two-tier green until a Committee member four putted, as a result of which the green was flattened.

Seven, which is uphill, is a decidedly better hole. It gets steadily better as we climb back to the highlands, and the second long shot lashed home, with an *oak tree to stymie us if we slice, is undeniably a good one.

* The oak tree, demolished by a flying bomb in World War II, was replaced by Bunny Millard in his Captain's year in 1954–55, slightly further right of centre than its predecessor. Thirty years later father and son are both doing well.

EIGHTH

484 yards, Bogey 5. The present Tenth played from a tee midway between present Ladies' Tenth tee and the reserve men's Tenth tee.

At the Eighth we are right back in the heather, and play a fine long straightforward hole, just a little too long for most of us to get home in 2.

NINTH

409 yards, Bogey 4. From the present Eleventh tee towards Coombe Hill to a green right of the present Eleventh green.

The Ninth sends us tacking downhill again with a pretty second shot to be played artistically with a little hook, just enough, let us suppose, to bring the ball curving gently round from the right, on a beautifully true keen green, and gradually dying away at the hole side.

TENTH

370 yards, Bogey 4. From 40 yards behind the top tee of the present Twelfth on a line to the houses beyond the present Sixth fairway (no longer visible because of the trees left of the present Twelfth fairway) to a green within Caesar's Camp – now the gorse area left of the fairway of the present Sixth.

A drive and a good long iron shot on to a perched up green, with a steep drop to the right, and stony ground at the bottom of it to punish a slice.

ELEVENTH

322 Yards, Bogey 4. Short walk down from Caesar's Camp to a tee on the left (as it is now played) of the Twelfth fairway. Drive to present Second green.

Then down the hill yet once more, whins and bracken to the right, a wood to the left, and a very 'kittle' pitch at the end of it between two sentinel bunkers. That is the end of the heather country for some while, more's the pity.

TWELFTH

150 yards, Bogey 3. Walk down the slope on left of present Twelfth green to the tee. Play across the present Third hole to a green surrounded by a horseshoe bank, now deep in the woods right of the present Third fairway.

Twelve is a short hole – a firm mashie shot on to a green ringed round with trouble.

THIRTEENTH

368 yards, Bogey 4. Tee near the boundary of the Course in the woods right of the Third fairway. Dogleg, with two hedges across fairway, and a duckpond to catch a sliced tee shot. Desirable to use a retrievable floater (Silver King) ball. The green in same position as present Third.

Thirteen has a good shoulder-opening drive over a dry dip that was once a pond [filled in by 1922], then up a hill.

FOURTEENTH

330 yards, Bogey 4. From the present Fourth tee over the shoulder of the hill (then without trees) on the right of the present Fourth fairway (then heavily wooded) towards the Practice Ground. Second shot back over ditch to a green near the present Ladies' Fifteenth tee.

Fourteen presents a great opportunity to the man who can hit a long drive with a hook, and a great opportunity for the adversary if he hooks a little too boldly [and lands in the ditch running across the present Fifteenth].

FIFTEENTH

416 yards, Bogey 5. From the present Ladies' Fifteenth tee to a green 50 yards beyond the present Fifteenth green.

Fifteen wants two very full wood shots on to a green rather above the player. It is a deceptive hole, for the green looks so close that we are always arrogantly taking irons, only to find that we could not have got up even with a driver.

SIXTEENTH

396 yards, Bogey 5. Walk forward to tee near the Wool Road boundary of the Course. A fine dogleg right. Tee shot left of poplars to set up the second shot to the present Sixteenth green.

Sixteenth is I think decidedly the most lovable of the lowland holes. It has a really joyous tee shot from a high place so that the ball appears to sail away a prodigious distance into the valley below.

SEVENTEENTH

304 yards, Bogey 4. Walk up hill through wood to Seventeenth tee short of the present Practice Bunker. Tee shot up the present Eighteenth fairway, a slice being blocked by the oak tree on the right (now rather larger than in 1920). Second shot to green in far corner of Cannizaro allotments.

The Seventeenth, though a very pretty little hole round the corner of some woodland, hardly carries enough guns for its situation in life.

EIGHTEENTH

214 yards, Bogey 4. Walk back to the Cannizaro boundary to Eighteenth tee by fir tree still standing there. A baffy (four wood) shot to a green in front of the Clubhouse, with a trough bunker on the verandah side.

Always seems to me a nerve-testing hole. People may say what they like about not ending with a short hole but if we are all square with one to play, do we relish having to hit a wooden club straight at a flag?

The old Eighteenth also tested the nerves of Members who had finished their round. Varying degrees of slice landed in the verandah, clattered on the Clubhouse roof, and at least on one occasion penetrated a window and holed out in the kitchen sink.

It took some years to get the new Course into shape. One of the Committee's first acts was to legislate for the protection of whins; but more costly measures were called for. Between 1911 and 1914 routine upkeep cost about £1,000 a year, whereas 'new work', which meant changing the original layout, took another £300 a year, imposing a considerable strain on the Club's resources. An increase in membership to meet increased costs had the predictable result – congestion at weekends, leading to a demand to reduce the membership; but the Club could not afford to lose subscriptions when costs were escalating.

The development of the Course continued even after the outbreak of war in 1914. A new Sixth green was made, drainage was improved, a mound between the Sixth and Seventh 'Courses' (ie fairways) was levelled, the Eleventh hole was given a new tee. This ended the work carried out by specially-engaged labour, and it was left to the ground staff to make any further changes. The pond on the Thirteenth fairway (now the Third) was filled in. 'Rough grasses' were experimented with – *Avia flexenosa* transplanted from Caesar's Camp, and Marram grass brought from Westward Ho!. The rough in front of the Fourth tee was improved to help the short driver. In the middle of the war, however, changes were designed to increase food production rather than the enjoyment of the golfers. (See Chapter 11: *Wars.*)

Now that Royal Wimbledon had its own Course its rights on the Common were a luxury; but, perhaps out of loyalty to their sister Club, they did not abandon the Common immediately. In December 1909 a joint Committee was set up to maintain the Common Course, each Club now being responsible

The Clubhouse area in 1923 showing the old Eighteenth Green with trough bunker in front of the verandah, and old Seventeenth Green to the right (now allotments).

for its own nine holes. From January 1910 costs were split three ways – between Royal Wimbledon, the London Scottish, and the newly-formed Wimbledon Town Club (later to become the Common Club). Then in October 1915 Royal Wimbledon told the others they regretted they must pull out. They would no longer contribute to the upkeep of the Common Course.

In the next few years changes were regularly made in the layout of the new Course, suggesting that perfection had not yet been achieved. Charles Ambrose, taking Royal Wimbledon as his text, held that Green Committees were incapable of designing a good course. They saw hopeless jungles, where a professional golf architect would see a first-class hole. The amateur could not visualize the effect of cutting down a whole wood. 'So he usually runs his holes over meadowland, which is always muddy and highly unsuitable for golf. That is what seems to have happened at Wimbledon. The Club has some really wonderful bits of golfing country on the wooded hillside below Caesar's Camp, but either it did not occur to them to use it, or they did not know how to. Then Mr Colt was sent for and things began to happen in all directions.'

It is difficult to decide how far this criticism is justified; but the ultimate responsibility must lie with the Committee. In 1919 the Captain, Stephen Fairbairn (the Australian oarsman), arranged at his own expense for a report by Harry Colt, the golf architect (a former member of the Club, and a fine golfer who had played on the Common), on the possible development of the Course. Extracts make interesting reading:

> I had not seen the present Course before yesterday, and was greatly surprised owing to what I had heard about it in the past when I saw the character of the class of land available for golf ... It appeared to me that it would be quite possible to construct 18 holes on the high ground without using the low lying valley, except for the purpose of 2 holes connecting Wimbledon Wood with the rest of the ground.
>
> The two high portions of land seemed to be sand and gravel and eminently suitable for a high class inland Course. The turf is just what is wanted for the game, although there is a certain amount of sorrel present ... There are many delightful natural features, and the views from the high ground are most attractive ... To have heather, bracken, beautiful birch woods, and gorse within a distance of less than eight miles from Hyde Park Corner, combined with an abundant supply of undulating ground furnished with many natural features suitable for the game, place the scheme in a class almost by itself ...
>
> On the existing Course there are several bad holes, which however could no doubt be greatly improved; and the artificial mounds and bunkers could also be altered on better landscape lines, so as to conform with the natural beauty of the surroundings ... I would strongly urge the Club to construct the best possible Course that could be made on the land available for the purpose, by using Wimbledon Wood and also Shadwell Wood for an 18-hole Course, and making use of the low-lying valley with heavy soil for a subsidiary 9- or 18-hole Course, which would be of great use on crowded days ...

Colt failed to persuade the Club to have a second Course, but his eighteen-hole layout was introduced in 1924 when elements of old and new Courses were in use at the same time. The most striking change was the replacement of the First hole (where virtually identical shots to the First green could produce anything from an eagle two to a multiple bogey) with the present dogleg right. A golfing journalist, who prefaced his remarks with the profound truth that 'a detailed description of holes, new or old, makes dull reading for golfers who have never played them', wrote: 'The old First hole was not lacking in individuality. But its character conformed to none of the canons of golfing orthodoxy. For the purpose of match play competitions, it was probably the worst in the world'. The same writer waxed lyrical about the new Course: 'By clearing away a big wood [where the Fourth fairway now is] the whole countryside has been opened up to the eye, and the imposing bunkers and built-up putting greens are in keeping with the sense of distance which lends enchantment to the scene'. The excellence of the layout underlined the wisdom of avoiding amateur designers.

The Course, which had cost just under £7,000, was formally opened in October 1924 when the Captain, Colonel G. A. Malcolm DSO, of the London Scottish Regiment, drove the first ball. There followed a match against the Oxford and Cambridge Golfing Society (see Chapter 15: *Matches*). It proved necessary in 1925 to bring back some of the old greens to rest the new. Successive Green Committees approved further modifications. For example, the programme of new work in 1929 included the construction of fifteen bunkers, filling in or modifying fourteen others, and making three new tees – suggesting that even the professional architect had failed to get things right first time.

In 1938 the Club was granted a 60-year lease from the Wimbledon Borough Council, which had acquired the freehold of the land. This security of tenure might have encouraged further modification, but it was not until 1945 and the end of World War II that it became practicable. Plans for reconstruction costing £3,000 were evolved, but only minor work was done. The principal changes since 1924 were at opposite ends of the Course: the loss of the green and tee by Beverley Brook beyond the present Ninth tee; the replacement of the Seventeenth (formerly played from the area of the present practice bunker to the ground now devoted to allotments) by the present short Seventeenth; and the inclusion of the present Eighteenth replacing its potentially lethal predecessor, with the green at a safer distance from the Clubhouse. Otherwise, the Course as it is played today remains broadly Colt's design.

Bernard Darwin was one who found the successive changes in the Course confusing. He wrote in 1947:

> I always enjoy going to Wimbledon. Everybody is so kind to me there. I remembered the roast beef at lunch from last year and it was just as exquisite this year. The Course itself is so engaging and never prettier than when the trees are clad in their autumnal yellows and browns. Moreover there was this year one particular source of pleasure, that I knew where I was and did not feel dizzy. The order of the holes has been so often changed there that I have of late years been completely 'done over and confoozled' in trying to relearn the numbers. Now they have resumed their old sequence, much as it was when Mr Colt first laid out the Course and I used often to play there. So once again I felt that my foot was on my native heath ... Altogether a lovely, lazy, friendly day.

As to the future, a 300-year lease from the Borough of Merton was recently secured for £300,000 with a peppercorn rent, and signed on 14 February 1986. The Club's former lease, due to expire in 2038, would have been subject to costly rent reviews.

Many Clubs have the professional talent among their Members to enable them to conclude such a deal, but the right men may not be in office at the right time. Costly errors can be made by amateurs and large fees paid to professional advisers. We were fortunate in that our negotiations extended over the Captaincy of John Bevan, Stanley Harding, and Sir Barry Sheen, upon whose combined skills – supported by Trustees Ian Bowie, Sir John Cradock-Hartopp, and Sir John Stocker, and two eminent property men, Alan Roberts and Bill Evans – it would have been difficult to improve.

The money was raised with the enthusiastic support of Members through a loan scheme in two parts. All full Members – except those of advanced years – put up a mandatory interest free loan of £200, and Five-day Members, of £120. The balance was raised through voluntary loans, with a maximum of £5,000, Members being entitled to a subscription discount of 6 per cent on their loans, indexed in line with future increases in subscription.

This simple but somewhat unusual loan scheme, with safeguards about the timing of repayments, avoids the pitfalls into which Clubs sometimes fall of granting Life Membership for sums which prove to be inadequate having regard to rising costs. The voluntary loan scheme was substantially oversubscribed and the two Extraordinary General Meetings called to approve it and the mandatory loans were both concluded in less than an hour – in happy contrast to the General Meeting described on page 15 which lasted off and on from 11 November 1880 to 3 February 1881.

Thanks to the foresight of the gentlemen listed above, their fellow Members and their descendants may now enjoy the amenities of Royal Wimbledon Golf Course unto the tenth generation.

Six

MEMBERS

IN NOVEMBER 1883, two years after opting for an independent existence, Royal Wimbledon took stock of their affairs at a General Meeting at Nicol's Café Royal Restaurant in Regent Street. In the discussion the relationship between finance and the number of Members predominated. A proposal to regard 30 overseas Members (who paid only 5s.0d. a year) as supernumerary and to increase the normal membership by 30 (to 350) and so ease the Club's financial position was opposed by many who thought it would lead to overcrowding. Dr Laidlaw Purves (who was to become Captain in 1897) claimed 'the game would hardly be worth the candle'. Far better to raise from two to three guineas the subscriptions of the 150 Members who had joined before March 1877 and still enjoyed their golf at the lower rate.

The differential subscription was a bone of contention for many years. At the General Meeting in April 1884 W. C. Anderson said it should be abolished. 'All those who came over from the Iron House fought the same battle, namely to get rid of the members of the Corps ... there was an implied understanding, when they all fought and won the battle in the interest of golf that they should all be on an equal footing.' The matter was raised and shelved at successive General Meetings but the problem diminished as the pre-1877 Members died off, and vanished when the last disappeared from the scene in the early 1920s.

Another perennial problem was what preferential treatment, if any, to give to local residents. In 1864 when the handful of the Rifle Volunteers formed their club there was no difficulty. So long as Earl Spencer blessed the project the aspirations of Wimbledon citizens were neither here nor there. When the Club was opened in 1869 to those living within three miles of the Windmill, and in 1871 to all-comers, it was on financial rather than good-neighbourly grounds; and when in the latter year residents had to pay a Common rate, they began to ask questions about the propriety of strangers playing golf on their land. The importance of remaining on good terms with the natives and of doing nothing to make more difficult the Conservators' task of holding the balance between the golfers and non-golfers was now self-evident.

When in December 1880 a group of ratepayers agitated about the increasing number of golfers, the Committee 'under the urgent nature of the circumstances' suspended all recruitment; but a month later deemed it so important 'to conciliate the people of the neighbourhood' that an exception was made in favour of candidates paying the Wimbledon Common rate and their sons over 18. Seven years later some Members suggested this arrangement should be formalized; but the Committee opposed the idea. It was ultimately agreed that until 1892 one ratepayer should be elected for every two outsiders.

The heavy expenditure in commissioning the new Course in 1907 necessitated an increase in full membership to 600. An average of 30 vacancies arose each year through resignation, death, and expulsion through failure to pay subscriptions; but there was every reason to believe the 600 target would be reached. Five-day Members were approved for the first time, with a maximum of 50. They had the right to play on any day except Saturdays, Sundays and Bank Holidays, and would be proposed and seconded in the ordinary way, but must come up for re-election annually.

These measures improved the financial position, but they were not enough. A £3,000 debenture issue was made in 1910 which increased indebtedness to over £6,000, to be reduced year by year through entrance fees. It was decided to ask any Member drawing a debenture of the previous issue to allow it to remain. A £1,000 overdraft was arranged with the London and South Western Bank. The Club survived well enough until World War I brought new difficulties. Subscription income was reduced by the numbers volunteering for active service, who then became Supernumerary Members paying nothing. In 1914, there were 585 Members – only 15 short of the 600 maximum aimed at in 1908 – but by the beginning of 1915 30 had departed on active service. A year later the number rose to 82, leaving only 472 paying Members, and leading to a very substantial drop in income. Moreover, the normal replacement rate slowed down dramatically. In March 1917, when the number of full Members had fallen to 436, the waiting list was reduced to a mere 2 – a serving officer and a prisoner of war, neither of whom, if elected, would have been liable for a subscription. A few years earlier there had been 150 on the waiting list.

Towards the end of 1918 things began to return to normal. Between January and November 1918 only 17 new Members were elected, but in December alone there were 10, and in the whole of 1919, 56. The Committee could now be more selective. It was not enough for a candidate to go forward on the strength of nomination and seconding. His sponsors were required positively to vouch for the suitability of their nominee, who must be a personal friend of long standing. Nationality and place of birth had to be stated on the nomination form, to ensure that no former enemy national was elected. A proposal that members of the clergy, birds of passage by profession, should be admitted with a reduced entrance fee, which might have been agreed in more difficult times, was turned down.

Montage of Members, 1892. (Presented by Sir John Greenborough.)

By the middle of 1919 the total membership of the Club had recovered to 515. 465 were paying the full subscription, which was graduated according to date of election. The differential in force in March 1877 still applied, to the benefit of 4 Members of more than 42 years standing. One unfortunate, elected in 1876, discovered in July 1919 that for those 42 years he had been paying a guinea a year too much. When he asked for his money back, the Committee begged him not to press the matter. 349 were paying five guineas, and 99 more recent Members, seven guineas. Although Members on active service need pay nothing, 20 had responded to an appeal to pay half the normal subscriptions.

For the next twenty years – to the eve of World War II – the membership arrangements remained unchanged, except for the periodical increases in entrance fees and subscriptions common to all Clubs. In 1938 the Wimbledon Borough Council acquired the freehold of the Course from Admiral the Honourable Sir R. Alexander R. Plunkett-Ernle-Erle-Drax. This cost far more than had been expected and the Club's new lease was correspondingly higher. It was believed that the financial position was secure, there being vacancies for 100 Members, (which if filled would substantially increase the Club's income); but it was nevertheless deemed prudent to institute a guarantee fund to cover the next five years. Members were asked to undertake in case of need to subscribe £1 a year; and they were invited to introduce suitable candidates to fill the vacancies.

A group of 18 Members, apprehensive about the financial implications of the change in ownership of the Course, took it upon themselves to do the Committee's job. They conducted their own investigation of the Club's catering services and submitted proposals for reducing costs. The Committee reacted vigorously. It pointed out to the 18 efficiency experts that they were elected to administer the Club's affairs so as to get the best out of Clubhouse and Course. Comparisons should not be made between running a Works Canteen for industrial welfare (of which several Committee members had considerable experience), or a restaurant for profit, and the provision for Members of the essential amenities they had the right to expect of a Club of the status of Royal Wimbledon. The Committee had noted that in the last 10 months the 18 dissidents had between them partaken of no more than 30 lunches. 'A very friendly feeling has always existed amongst the Members of the Club, which your Committee are desirous of maintaining and fostering – consequently they are very averse to adopting any drastic policy which might interfere with this atmosphere.' Finally, if Members took full advantage of the facilities offered by the Club there was no need for apprehension as to future finance. A copy of this chilling missive was sent to all the signatories of the memorandum.

In 1957 there were 369 full Members, 48 Five-day, 37 House and Country, 31 Honorary and Life, and 6 Clergy, whose prayers for a reduced subscription had been answered. There were 157 Members of the Ladies' Section. By 1965 a waiting list had developed, and as the Club was faced with heavy expenditure

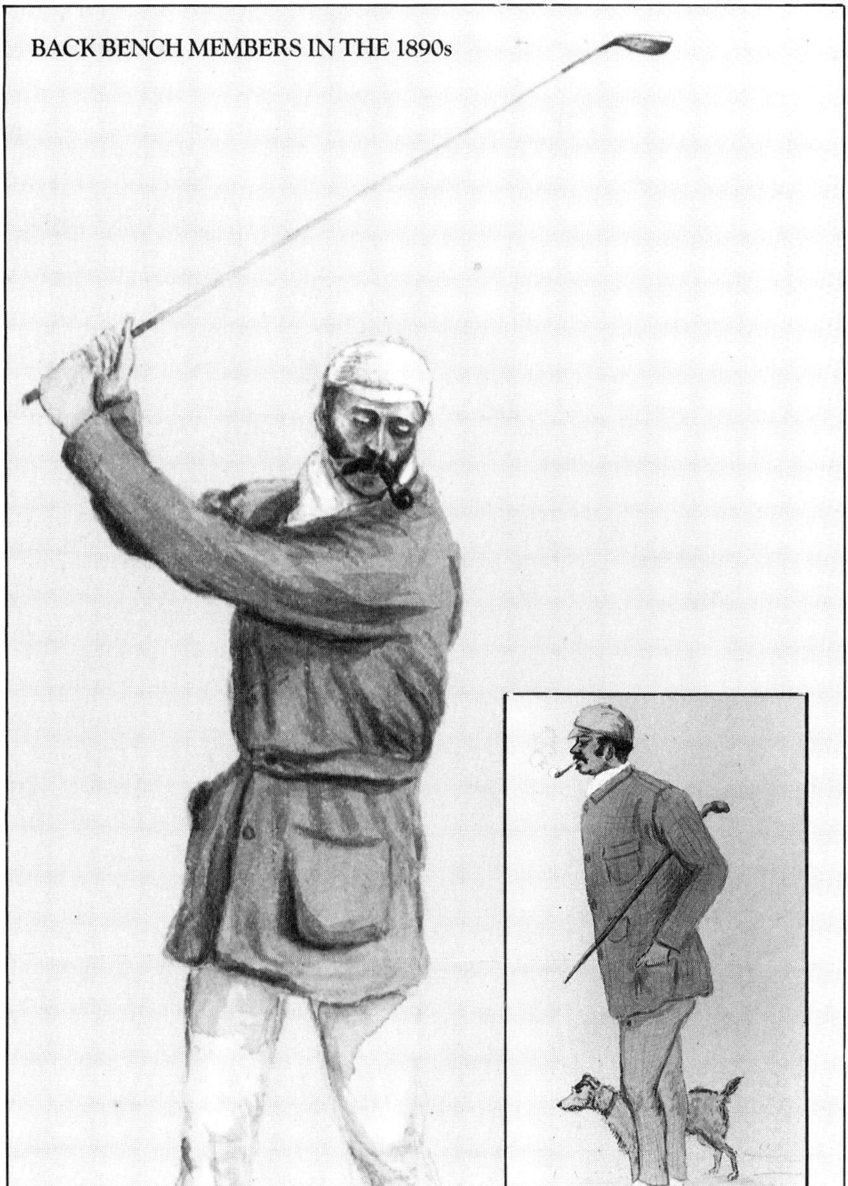

A.H. Molesworth and (inset) A.A. Steward

BACK BENCH MEMBERS IN THE 1890s

T.S. Henry and (inset) Felix Skene

on the Clubhouse a considerable number of new Members were elected. The waiting list is a necessary evil in all Clubs worthy of the name. Proficiency in golf may shorten it; but that it is not the sole criterion was argued by the sponsors of one who will never rival Sandy Lyle. They pointed out that time spent in bunkers and executing air shots would be made up by his 'fleetness of foot' from tee to green. Impressed by this argument, the Committee elected the candidate. His name? Sir Roger Bannister.

Members come from every profession, with medicine and law in the forefront. In the nineteenth century the Club was popular with members of parliament – at one time Thursday was chosen as a 'play day' since the Commons did not sit on that day. It is surprising that in those affluent times, with their Victorian values, so many Members were struck off the roll for failing to pay subscriptions. True, difficulty of communication could be a problem. Mr Cumming Macdona MP, the extrovert champion of lady golfers, lost his membership when he failed to pay his subscription in 1886, but he was reinstated when in March 1887 the Club received a letter from San Antonio in Texas explaining that he 'had been travelling through the Wild West for several months' and had for all practical purposes been incommunicado. Another was forgiven in similar circumstances having been caught out by the long trip to and from New Zealand.

From the earliest times the Club has welcomed golfers from overseas. First, those from Clubs scattered round the Empire, in particular in India; and then as golf infiltrated into Europe and the United States from the new Clubs there. Trophies were exchanged with some. In June 1887 the Bombay Golf Club presented the Club with a trophy still competed for, and were given a medal in return. The Wellington Bowl, presented by that friendliest of Clubs, the Wellington Golf Club, Heretaunga, New Zealand (founded by women, who graciously admitted men, with whom they still share equal rights), is appropriately the trophy for a mixed foursome competition. In 1947, when rationing was still a problem in Britain, the Ladies of Heretaunga sent 100 food parcels for the 100 most senior members of the Ladies' Section. In return the Section presented them with a silver salver engraved with the Windmill which is still competed for as the Wimbledon Salver. More recently the courtesy of the Course has been offered to Ambassadors to the Court of St James and Commonwealth High Commissioners, many of whom have accepted the offer with gratitude. In the last ten years the Club has been happy to receive players from the United States, France, Sweden, Belgium, Australia, South Korea, Hong Kong, Zimbabwe, Spain, Norway, Canada, Holland, Japan, France, Switzerland, Northern Ireland, Eire, India, Finland, and Pakistan. Reciprocal playing rights exist with leading Clubs in Canada, Australia, India, and Sri Lanka.

In August 1946 the Secretary proposed that the Club should make the Course available to Artisans; and in September 1947 the rules of a newly-formed Artisan Golfer Section were submitted for approval by the Committee. Membership was restricted to 36, 6 places at that time being reserved for

Caddies working at Royal Wimbledon. Artisans were required to start before 8.45 am on Saturdays and Sundays during the winter months, and after 3.15 pm. The Artisans, who provide a valuable service by organizing divotting parties twice a year, have many low-handicap players, and have had considerable success in the national Artisan competitions.

The first reference to a Club Dinner (if the dinners at the Dog and Fox, Wimbledon after the Blackheath matches are excepted) is in 1873 when Members dined together on the last day of the Autumn Meeting 'at some convenient place' – the Cannon Street Hotel, E.C. – suggesting there were more London than Wimbledon Members. Tickets (including sherry during dinner) 10s.6d., guests being allowed. The Annual General Meeting was held a week later at the Guildhall Tavern, where Members 'dined together at 7 o'clock at a cost of 5s.0d. each for the dinner'. Perhaps these functions were not well patronized for the Spring Meeting Dinner in 1874 was to be held only if a sufficient number applied, and there is no record that they did. There was no formal Dinner after the Autumn Meeting in 1874, but Members were told they could dine at the Fox and Hounds, Putney, giving two days' notice. In November 1875 the room at the Guildford Tavern 'usually taken for the annual dinner' was not available (showing there had been more than one dinner there) and instead the Criterion or St James's Hall were nominated.

Although the Club occupied Camp Cottage from 1882 the Annual Dinner was still held in London after the Autumn Meeting, in November 1884 at the Café Royal, Regent Street. It proved a success in every way. 'The Chair was occupied by ex-Captain Taylor, and Captain Guy Pym in succession, and under their genial sway, a most delightful evening was spent in listening to singing that was generally exceptionally good, and it was to all quite a disappointing surprise to find how suddenly the hour of parting had come.' In 1886 it was announced that 'A CLUB DINNER will be held in the Club House, Wimbledon on Saturday the 17th April at 7 o'clock pm, when it is hoped that the Captain, Mr John Murray Junior, will preside and present the prizes'. The price would now be 4s.6d., a considerable improvement on the Cannon Street Hotel, and even the Guildhall Tavern. In fact the Dinner was held on Saturday 24 April 1886. Since then Club Dinners have as a rule been held in the Clubhouse after the Spring and Autumn Meetings.

Singing seems to have been popular in the early days, no doubt stimulated by the drams and skirl of the pipes accompanying the haggis – the last a tradition stubbornly retained, although the Scottish element in the Club has been diluted since 1864. The haggis presented a problem in post-war austerity. It was necessary to get special permission from the Local Food Controller before this delicacy could be served. Entertainers have been employed from time to time with varying degrees of success, but in 1931 'it was decided to do without the services of a Professional Entertainer and the Secretary was asked to try to find Members willing to sing' – possibly for their supper. There were no volunteers. Entertainers have now been dropped in favour of the after-dinner speech, of which the Club boasts brilliant exponents. Dinners may be rather staider than they once were. There are tales (no doubt apocryphal) of diners in earlier times finding themselves in difficulty as they drove home: of one who butted the Bentley in front thrice at hundred yard intervals before the owner (not a Club Member) got out and politely indicated that enough was enough; and of another who accomplished the difficult feat of navigating his car to the middle of the Common Pond, whence he waded home, wetter and wiser. It may be truthfully said of the present Members that they are *sans peur et sans reproche*, models of decorum. No longer do they interrupt the Club Dinner to follow the piper (Colonel Douglas Grant MC of the London Scottish Regiment), like the entranced children of Hamelin, down the First fairway, round the First green, and back to the Dining Room in time for the presentation of prizes.

The Club celebrated its Centenary in 1965 with an ambitious programme of special events. On 26 May there was a 24-a-side match against Royal St George's, properly regarded as a daughter Club, having been founded by Laidlaw Purves and Henry Lamb. They set out from Royal Wimbledon to find terrain suitable for a Links Course within easy reach (as Elcho had done before them at Felixstowe), and lit on Sandwich, where Purves laid out the original Course. The mother Club won and in honour of the occasion at the dinner afterwards (attended by two former Amateur Champions, Roger Wethered and Cyril Tolley) presented daughter with a handsome silver miniature of the Windmill. This was accepted on her behalf by Special Agent 008 – alias Donald Smith, who had succeeded to the Captaincy of Royal St George's on the death of Ian Fleming, creator of 007 – and has a place of honour among the trophies in the Clubhouse at Sandwich. 008 presented the Royal Wimbledon with a replica of the Royal St George's exquisite Grand Challenge Vase, now on display in the Dining Room. Edward Scudamore gave an account of the ties between the two Clubs, including the sale to Royal Wimbledon Members of cheap rail tickets to Sandwich at the Royal Wimbledon bar, and the use of the Card Room for early St George's Committee Meetings.

On 18 June there was a Club Ball at Hurlingham attended by 250 Members and guests; and next day a foursomes scratch Invitation Tournament in which pairs from fifty leading Clubs took part. They included Royal Clubs in Britain, overseas Royals, Sunningdale, Walton Heath, Wentworth, The Honourable Company of Edinburgh Golfers, Prestwick, the Oxford and Cambridge Golfing Society, the Lucifers (the Commonwealth Golfing Society), and the Seniors. There had been apprehension about coping with such a major enterprise, but everything went perfectly, and the weather was kind. The Seniors' pair, John Beck and Alan Cave, won with a round of 75, defeating a very powerful field. (Royal Wimbledon, fearful they might have the bad taste to win their own competition, had not entered.) The trophy, a replica of the Silver Windmill, now resides at Woking, home of the Seniors.

There was a triangular three-ball sixsome with Royal Blackheath, opponents of a century earlier, and the neighbouring London Scottish, on 15 July. Eighteen holes of the Common Course in the morning, lunch with the London

Scottish, eighteen holes on the Royal Wimbledon Course in the afternoon, followed by dinner in the Clubhouse. The Club were the winners.

The principal event of the Centenary Year was the Autumn Dinner, held in the Savoy Ball Room, on 28 October – a splendid occasion attended by 440, including the Captain of the Royal and Ancient, J. L. Mitchell; Gerald Micklem, President of the English Golf Union; Michael Bonallack, the Amateur Champion, and many other distinguished figures from the world of golf. Since the Dinner doubled for the Captain's inaugural Dinner (normally held earlier in the year) the Captain's Chair was installed at the top table, which bore many of the Club's trophies, including the Silver Club and Balls. The Chair was first occupied by the outgoing Captain, W. Lister Barber, and vacated for his successor, Sir John Cradock-Hartopp Bt. These two, resplendent in their traditional red coats were, as befits good hosts, ensuring that all was in order before their guests arrived, when they were accosted by the Head Waiter, anxious to know which of them was the Toastmaster for this particular function. The Captain-elect regrets to this day that he failed to nominate his predecessor.

The Captain welcomed the in-coming Captain. The Club was proposed by the Captain of the Royal and Ancient, and replied to by Sir John Hartopp, who in the last few minutes had become Captain. The Guests were proposed by Commander James Allan, Captain 1971–72, the reply being made by Henry Longhurst.

One other important post-war event must be recorded – the appointment in 1977 of a special Planning and Development Committee 'to examine in the light of changes affecting golf Clubs generally, and the renewal of the Club's lease of the Course for sixty years, the objectives and services of the Club, its administrative structure and financial position, and the scope for improvements in the Clubhouse'. The Committee, under the Chairmanship of Stanley Harding, Captain in 1984–85, set about its task with the dedication of a Royal Commission, and took evidence from any Member who had suggestions to make. The importance of the Committee, on which the Ladies' Section was represented by their immediate Past Captain, Maire Cruickshank, lies not so much in its recommendations, many of which were implemented, as in the fact that the Club countenanced a thorough self-examination with a view to change, which Lord Elcho would certainly have vetoed had he still been President.

Seven

CAPTAINS

THE CAPTAIN OF A GOLF CLUB is the nearest thing to the Almighty you will meet on this earth. He will of course deny it, but it is true. The peculiar importance of the Captain was early recognized by Royal Wimbledon. In November 1882 two members, Alexander and Francis Crawford, gave the Club a Silver Golf Club, subject to these conditions:

> 1. That it be played for yearly by the Captain elect ... by playing a round of the Common, or hitting a ball off the first tee towards the first hole on the Medal Day thereby winning the Silver Club, and proving himself to be a golfer.
>
> 2. That each Captain shall add a ball to the Silver Club with his name and date of having won the Silver Club upon it.
>
> 3. That the Silver Club be placed on the Table in front of the Captain or his representative in the Chair for the time being at each half-yearly Dinner as a symbol of his position and authority.
>
> 4. That there shall never be a procession of the Silver Club or Balls nor any kissing of the Silver Club or Balls and that no other ceremony whatever shall take place either directly or indirectly connected with the Silver Club or the Balls attached thereto.
>
> 5. That in the event of the Royal Wimbledon Golf Club being broken up or ceasing to exist as a golf club as at present constituted the Silver Club and Balls shall be and remain the absolute property of us or the successor of us his executors, administrators, or assigns.

The fourth condition – that the Silver Club shall never be carried in procession and that there shall be no kissing of the Club or Balls – is interesting. In imposing it the Crawfords saved Royal Wimbledon from plagiarising the ceremonial of the Royal and Ancient. The Silver Club is still placed before the Captain at Club Dinners, but no Silver Ball has been added since 1938–39 – a sad break with tradition.

Photographs of Royal Wimbledon Captains march round the Clubhouse. The current holder of the office maintains a benevolent surveillance of activities at the Nineteenth Hole, until at his year's end he is carried off to bring up the rear of the endless queue winding through labyrinthine corridors to the Committee Room, where the destinies of the Club are shaped, and where twenty-six of the earliest Captains give silent blessing to the decisions of their distant successors.

Scrutiny of these faces – which will take you upwards of two hours – revives the unanswerable question: Why do men so different in character and profession, become addicted to the game of golf? There is no physiognommical common factor, other than funereal solemnity in the early days, to hint at an explanation. This suggests that most saw golf as a second religion, much as New Zealanders see rugby football as their first. True, no smile could penetrate the early beards and walrus moustaches but the camera can pick up a twinkle. Yet it is not until the 1950s, eighty Captains on, that there is the vestige of a smile. Then, curiously enough, there is a succession of six who, if the camera tells the truth, found life or golf or both highly amusing.

This raises another question. How did the early stalwarts conduct themselves as they played their rounds, first seven holes, and later the statutory eighteen? Did they carry the solemnity of the photographic record on to the First tee, and devote their entire attention to playing the game? Was conversation limited to a tight-lipped 'Your hole, Sir' and an occasional grudging 'Good shot, Sir'? Was defeat a tragedy to be brooded on for the rest of the week?

True, the early Captains are an inadequate sample. They were better golfers than the back bench members, and therefore more serious. The levity with which golf is now played is in direct proportion to the players' incompetence; but in the beginning even the incompetent rank and file saw victory as a matter of life and death. Many disputes might well have been settled by a duel under the shadow of the Windmill with weapons more lethal than a baffy or mashie-niblick.

The evidence of the early Captains' faces, therefore, supported by the ordinary Members' grim approach, suggests a change in the Club's first century, surely for the better – in spite of Bernard Darwin's approval of sentiments from 'the depth of J. H. Taylor's soul': 'I like to see a player settle down to his job with determination, and have little patience with those who enter upon it in the spirit of a picnic. To try to play golf really well is far from being a joke, and light-heartedness of effort is a sure sign of eventual failure'. O.K. Spoken like an Open Champion, eye on rewards beyond the dreams of avarice. But we cannot all be Open Champions. We cannot blame the club golfer who approaches the First tee on a Saturday morning, sights firmly set on 50 pence, showing less determination than the Taylors and Ballesteroses, and with a mind not entirely closed to the picnic at the Nineteenth, in the congenial company of non-Taylors and non-Ballesteroses.

If we are to examine the career of one Captain – and space hardly permits 104 biographies – the choice must fall on Dr William Laidlaw Purves, Captain in 1897–1898, not because he achieved most – although he did achieve a great deal – but because he is the most interesting.

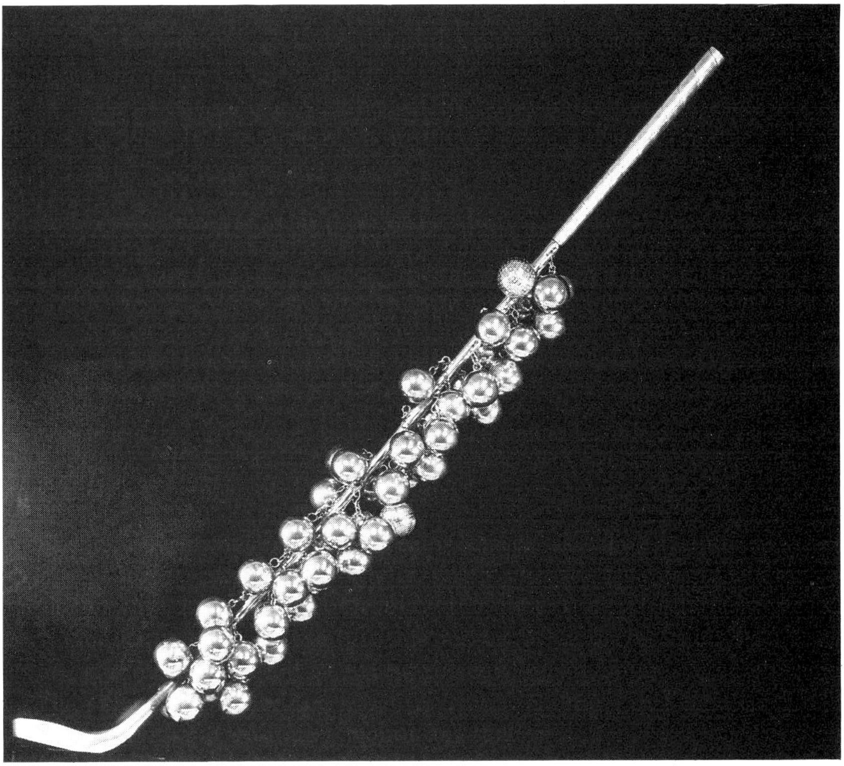

The Silver Club presented in 1882 by Alexander and Francis Crawford, to which successive Captains have added a Silver Ball.

Born in Edinburgh in 1843, he was educated at the High School and University there. He studied law, but changed to his father's profession of medicine, graduating MD in 1864. He continued his studies abroad and in 1874 settled in London where he became lecturer and consultant surgeon at Guy's Hospital. Earlier he had served as doctor on a whaling ship, and spent three years in Australia.

He was elected to the Club in 1874, and two years later was involved in a major row about marking his partner's card. After hearing both sides, and taking evidence from a third party, the Committee recorded that 'the full statements of the parties ... are of so conflicting a nature that the Committee is unable to decide the whole question on its merits. Taking however each party's case on his own representation, the Committee consider there was no warrant for such hasty inferences on both sides, or such loss of temper as was evidently displayed on one'. Nothing Dr Purves said justified the construction put on it or the strong epithets used; but Dr Purves 'ought to have stated his objection before the ball was played, not after the hole had been played out'. He had knowingly allowed his partner to break a rule, and strong epithets were certainly justified. All this might suggest that he should not attain high office.

He quickly came to the forefront as a golfer, playing regularly in Club competitions. He won the aggregate prize for the 3 rounds of the Autumn Meeting in 1876, with 86, 85, and 90, off scratch; his 85 winning him third place and a dozen balls in the handicap competition. During his playing career he won most of the Club's major trophies, including the Silver Shield, Silver Iron (with Norman Foster), the Kennard Medal, the Anderson Beakers, the Ridpath Challenge Bowl, and – twice – the Club Gold Medal. He won his last trophy, the Ridpath Challenge Bowl, in 1914 at the age of 71 (when his handicap was 3) with a net 74.

In 1883 he joined the Committee, and took an active part in its business, although he was more interested in the game than in administration. In particular he was obsessed by the rules, not yet codified and nationally accepted, and took the lead in evolving the Royal Wimbledon version. (See Chapter 13: *Rules*.) In November 1885 he supported a proposal to play the Course 'the reverse way' which was approved subject to the agreement of the London Scottish, with whom Royal Wimbledon shared the Common Course. (There would have been problems had one Club continued to follow the orthodox route while the other went widdershins.) Shortly afterwards he resigned from the Committee to make more time for professional literary work.

He was appointed Captain in 1897. It was appropriate that his first problem should involve the rule about whins. (The treatment of whins and the price of tea, bread and butter are recurrent themes in the Club records.) The penalty for lifting from a whin was two strokes. That for lifting from a rabbit scrape, one. But when the rabbit scrape was within a whin, what then? Did both penalties apply? After considerable discussion (there was always considerable discussion) it was decided, illogically, that the penalty for the combined misfortune was one stroke.

A quiet Captain's year followed. No financial problems. No need to levy forced loans from Members. No acceleration of recruitment of Members to balance the books, or slowing it to avoid overcrowding. No battles with the Conservators about golfers' rights on the Common. No civil war with Members of the London Scottish. No quest for a new Clubhouse. Comparative peace from the non-golfers of Wimbledon and Putney. The only real problem was Course maintenance for which the recently-appointed Professional, J. H. Taylor, was responsible. He, an Open Champion, was more interested in the financial rewards of the game than in a Greenkeeper's job, and allowed the Course to suffer in spite of the admonitions of Purves and his Committee.

In the years after his Captaincy Purves lost the respect of his confrères. He regularly made suggestions, ranging from minor matters, say meal charges, to major questions of Club policy, all of which successive Committees allowed to lie on the table. When a General Meeting decided to raise subscriptions his protests were ignored. He spent a great deal of time in 1907 designing the new Course and no doubt making use of the experience he had gained laying out

Royal St George's, Sandwich, twenty years earlier. Having presented his plan to the Committee, he withdrew to allow them to discuss it freely. They 'came to the conclusion that it would be advisable to have a professional to go over the Course after it was marked out by Purves, as it was a matter of such vital importance'. When Purves heard the verdict he was clearly upset. 'He said he must consider this point, and retired.'

The club went ahead with its plan to employ a professional architect; and the Secretary, Norman Foster, wrote a mollifying letter to the aggrieved Purves:

> Dear Purves,
> Regarding what I said to you in Committee today about our being unable to criticise your plans of the Course, we were sorry that the suggestion to abdicate in favour of a professional should have made you hesitate. I am sure you will believe that this wish on the Committee's part is not from any doubt of your absolute ability to perform the task without any assistance, but we have to consider outside opinion, which perhaps does not know you so well, and we have heard it from so many sides that the opinion of a professional was desirable that we cannot very well ignore this feeling . . .

Purves was not to be mollified. His reply was brief and to the point:

> Dear Foster,
> The enclosed [maps] may be of use to the Club. They are not of any further service to me. The outlay of money I have made, I give to the Club. The time I have expended is more serious . . .

The Committee made one more attempt at mollification. They assured Purves they much appreciated his kindness in volunteering to lay out the Course, and recognized that he was better qualified than any professional. 'Please let that be accepted as absolutely sincere.' That they were calling in a professional to revise his plan did not imply doubt about its merits. It was simply that everything must be done to ensure the best possible Course. All to no avail. Purves would have nothing more to do with the project. Other snubs followed in regular succession, and his later years at Wimbledon, where he took a house near the Common, cannot have been very happy.

Perhaps his greatest contributions to golf were the part he played with Henry Lamb and other Members of Royal Wimbledon in founding and designing the Royal St George's Club at Sandwich, where many Open Championships have been held, and his successful efforts in 1890 to revive the Wimbledon Ladies' Golf Club, first formed in 1872. (See Chapter 16: *Ladies*.) The latter achievement was recognized in some highly forgettable lines recited by Mr Webster Glynes when Purves was presented with his portrait at a ceremony at Royal St George's:

> At Wimbledon, Ladies he encouraged to play;
> And now they progress in a marvellous way.

The successful reborn Wimbledon Ladies' Club, in which the driving force was the formidable Issette Pearson, became the progenitor of the Ladies' Golf

J. Lionel Ridpath, 1887-88

Dr W. Laidlaw Purves, 1897-98

CAPTAINS

E.C. Millard, 1954-55

The Hon. Sir Barry Sheen, 1985-86

Union. Miss Pearson paid her tribute to Purves in *The Golfing Annual* in rather more memorable prose than Mr Glynes's verse:

> The idea of a Ladies' Golf Union originated with some half-dozen members of the Wimbledon Ladies' Golf Club, who expressed a wish to establish an Open Championship for ladies. The wish was communicated to Mr W. Laidlaw Purves, who warmly took up the subject, and under his guidance notices were sent to all the Ladies' Clubs to ascertain what support would be given.

The result was most encouraging, and in April 1893 Purves presided over a meeting of 32 delegates from the 15 leading Ladies' Clubs. He stressed the importance of an authority to make rules for the Ladies' game, to facilitate inter-club and international matches, and a Ladies' Championship.

The Ladies' Golf Union was an instant success and went from strength to strength; and the Ladies showed their appreciation of Purves's efforts on their behalf by making him one of their four Vice-Presidents.

Why did Purves not mature into an elder statesman whose views were respected and whose wishes the Club would strain every nerve to meet? He was a first-class golfer, dedicated to the game and to the needs of Royal Wimbledon as he saw them. Yet it seems he ceased to be accepted by his fellow Members. During the Club's appeal to the First Commissioner of Works against the regulations proposed in 1909, he made his own representations, when he might have been expected to support the Club's petition. His case was that a green fee would hit the poorer classes, among whom he almost seemed to include himself. He pointed out that he had four sons and two daughters, all golfers, and that every round his family played would cost him 7s.0d. on top of the Common rate, although it was hardly the Conservators' fault that he had rendered himself liable to finance seven golfers.

Perhaps his enthusiasm for women's golf was deprecated by those Members of Royal Wimbledon who welcomed women in the kitchen or bedroom, but saw no place for them on the Links. Or his bad temper may have had something to do with it. When Edward Scudamore feared his references to the irascible Purves in *The Early Days of Golf at Wimbledon* might hurt his daughter Lady Swann (who received a copy from Cecil Leitch), she wrote: 'No, between you and me he was (with a heart of gold) the most irascible man I ever met!' As a young girl Lady Swann helped him when he was working on the Ladies' Course. 'I have vivid recollections of my Father laying out the Ladies' nine-hole Course, when I held the measuring chain as we went from green to green.'

Purves proposed a new handicapping scheme in October 1912. He tabulated every score in every competition over three years, and based handicaps on the difference between the average of the player's three best scores, nine of which had to be in Medal competitions, and the par of the Course. The Committee said his scheme 'was impossible to work ... but was admirable otherwise'. Because of his great labour his proposal could not decently lie on the table. It was eventually decided 'that the system of tabulation recommended by Dr Purves be adopted' but for guidance only. The

Handicapping Committee fell back on the time-honoured system of looking at cards and listening to Nineteenth Hole grumbling by aggrieved losers – which gave universal satisfaction before the present computerized system that takes an Einstein to comprehend it, and a Paul Getty to finance the entrance fees needed to add a single shot to a handicap.

Purves was an all-rounder. In addition to his medical writings, he wrote on Daniel Defoe, and made translations from French to English. He died at his home, Hardwicke Cottage, Wimbledon Common, on 30 December 1918, aged 75.

Three other Captains must be mentioned: Henry Lamb, Norman Foster, and the Prince of Wales, later King Edward VIII.

Henry Lamb joined the Club in 1873, and served as Honorary Secretary from 1877–1890. He was elected Captain in 1890, and died three years later. His great influence on the affairs of the Club, particularly during the difficult days of the split with the London Scottish Club, emerges clearly from the records. His portrait, painted when he was elected a Life Member in 1891, hangs in the Dining Room. He was succeeded as Secretary by Norman Foster, who served until 1900, when a Professional Secretary was appointed. Foster became Captain in 1906, and was a Trustee from 1908 until the year of his death, 1937. No-one ever served a Club more faithfully.

The Prince of Wales, a keen golfer, played frequently at Royal Wimbledon, usually in the morning when the Course was empty. He had lessons from the Professional, Fred Leach, and used clubs made by the Assistant Professional, Spen Attwood, now Professional at the London Scottish, where he still makes clubs. It is recorded on 3 March 1928 that 'TRH The Prince of Wales, and The Duke of York having expressed a desire to become Honorary Members of the Club, the Secretary was instructed to place their nominations on the agenda for the Spring General Meeting'. Edward accepted the Captaincy in 1928–1929.

He presided at the Spring Meeting Dinner, wearing the traditional Captain's red tail coat. Although there was great interest in the event, the number of diners was not increased. Committee, Past Captains, and prize winners had preference, and a ballot held for the other places. Mr Leigh-Ibbs had the task of hiring suitable entertainers. (Their contribution sometimes bordered on the indelicate, so that waitresses were required to withdraw; but a surviving witness records that, no doubt owing to the acoustics of the Iron Room, now the Dining Room, this precaution generally failed.) A Past Captain present on this special occasion remembers nothing to bring a blush to the cheeks of the most innocent waitress. The Silver Club was handed to the Prince (with the latest ball bearing his name) by the immediate Past Captain, Dr R. Worth, who proposed the health of his successor, who had taken part in the Meeting and had missed the major handicap prize by a single shot thanks to four putts on the Eighteenth green. The Prince's own speech revealed his great affection for the Course and the Club.

Unhappily, being unfamiliar with the rules, he was later accompanied on the

Course by a lady not a member of the Club. A gentleman Member, a true democrat, drew his attention to the fact that the convention that the Crown can do no wrong did not apply on the golf course. The Prince finished the round, but made it his last at Royal Wimbledon. That he bore no grudge is witnessed by the fact that he later consented to be President from 1931–1935.

Up to the present (1986) the Club has had 104 Captains – the office being held at some periods for more than one year. Three were also Captains of the Royal and Ancient at some stage in their golfing career: Sir Robert Finlay in 1903; Brigadier General Sir David Kinloch Bt. (1905); and The Prince of Wales (1922). Ten other Members of the Club have captained the R and A, including Field Marshall Earl Haig (1920); The Duke of York (1930); Bernard Darwin (1934); and Roger Wethered (1946).

If the Captain of a Golf Club approximates to the Almighty it is difficult to know where in the cosmology to place the Trustees, those gentlemen who hold in trust the Course and Clubhouse and all that in them is. It is an understatement to say they play the House of Lords to the Committee's Commons. Where their orbits intersect is all knowledge of golf club administration. The present trio, who have devoted years of service to the Club, first on the Committee, then as Captain, embody a wide range of experience. A distinguished accountant who formerly guided the fortunes of one of the country's leading firms and who, like many of the Club's founder Members, is an immigrant from the home of golf. A prominent industrialist and brilliant golfer – semi-finalist in the English Amateur Championship. An Appellate Judge, whose performances on the fairway and in the rough are unreliable indicators of his abilities on the Bench and in the Committee Room.

The Trustees, like the brook, go on forever, although they chatter less. They influence the affairs of the Club longer than the Captain, who though godlike, is ephemeral. But there are exceptions. The Captain for 1984–85 miraculously succeeded in influencing the affairs of the Club for three centuries to come, a record that is unlikely to be beaten. Had he been elected three centuries ago, we would today be reaping the reward of his foresight, owners of our Course as well as our Clubhouse.

All Captains hope to do something for posterity. Not all succeed. One who has the honour to be a Trustee sadly remembers his sole achievement in a year of financial stringency: the improvement – after months of pleading – of the lighting in his dingy changing room by upgrading a 60-watt bulb to 100-watts. At least he tried.

Eight

PROFESSIONALS

ROYAL WIMBLEDON has had sixteen Professionals.

The first was Doleman, a member of London Scottish Rifle Volunteers, employed part time, and described as 'club maker and instructor'. The arrangement which continued until 1869 was that he should supply clubs and balls, and carry out repairs according to an agreed tariff. When he was not engaged at the Butts he was available to play with Members at 2s.0d. for the first 2 rounds (that is of the seven-hole Course), or less than 2 rounds, and 1s.0d. for every subsequent round. However, if a Member wanted his services when he was on duty, they could be secured at the same rates plus 3s.0d. to hire a substitute at the Butts – with the implication that the requirements of golfers took precedence over the defence of the realm. In 1869 it was proposed to ask the Commanding Officer to approve the engagement of Doleman during the winter months at 18s.0d. a week, but then it was felt that a full-time Professional was called for.

In May 1870 applications for the post were considered. Not surprisingly the Committee 'took a favourable view of Young Tom Morris's application' – he having already won the second of his four successive Open Championships – but they decided to wait until September, then the beginning of the golfing year, before making an appointment. In the event Tom Dunn was appointed 'Professional Golf Club and Ball Maker', one of his duties being to supervise the cleaning of clubs, surely inappropriate for a great champion. When the Course was extended from seven to eighteen holes in February 1871 Dunn was instructed to 'pick out some new holes'. (See Chapter 5: *Courses*.) Before long his 20s.0d. a week, and the failure of many to pay their subscriptions, put the Club in the red; but several Members undertook to make good the deficiency.

The Club asked that Dunn should be allowed to use one of the Conservators' sheds as a workshop, and have the tenancy of the first cottage falling vacant at the Windmill. More optimistically they suggested he should act as a Special Constable, as he would be constantly on the Common, well placed to be of material service in the preservation of order. The Conservators agreed about the shed and that he should have the first refusal of the next Windmill cottage to become available, but the idea that he should become a Special Constable was politely rejected. He continued to give loyal service, and in 1880 his salary was increased to 25s.0d. a week. He was also given a bonus of £10 for his help in transferring the Club's property from the London Scottish Iron House to their new premises in Camp Road. In October 1877 he played a 36-hole match against the great Tom Morris. (See Chapter 15: *Matches*.)

He was succeeded in 1881 by John Thomson, engaged to work as club maker on his own account. The Club gave him an advance to start him off, and Members were asked to pay cash for balls, clubs and repairs. Things did not go well, and three years later there was no sign that Thomson would ever pay off his loan. He claimed in February that he was owed £40, and that if Members would settle their bills he could reduce his debt by £16 before the end of the year. The Secretary helped him by drafting a letter inviting prompt payment, but the real trouble was that he was a poor craftsman as well as a poor businessman. In 1886 the Secretary of the London Scottish complained that their clubmaker was being swamped by orders from the Royal Wimbledon, which led the Committee to conclude: 'that a better man should be got if the Club desired to obtain the position to which it was in every way entitled to aspire'. It was decided to employ a paid servant instead of the semi-independent Thomson, who would under the Green Committee supervise the Course, take charge of the caddies, and make clubs and balls. Thomson was told that if he did not get the job, he would have to go.

The Club's advertisement in *The Field* for a replacement produced ten interesting applications: from Thomson himself, who in the circumstances cannot have had much hope of success; Alexander Patrick of Leven; Peter Paxton of Malvern; George Lowe of Hoylake; Charles Gibson of North Berwick; Willie Park Jr. of Musselburgh; William Scott Fernie of Felixstowe; A. Walker of Southport; John Patrick of Dunbar; and finally John Butchart of The London Scottish Golf Club (who had in effect been doing Thomson's job for him) – a field which suggests that the Royal Wimbledon was held in the highest esteem by leading Professionals throughout the country.

They all had excellent testimonials, which made the choice difficult, but after serious consideration the Committee unanimously decided 'that Alexander Patrick of Leven was in every respect the most suitable for the situation'. He was offered 30s.0d. a week and a free shop, and took up the post the first week of October 1886. In the following year he was granted leave of absence in July and August (presumably to take part in professional tournaments) on condition that his brother took his place, and was fully instructed about the management of the Course. Early in 1891 Patrick announced that he wanted to return to Leven after the Spring Meeting, and suggested that he be replaced by his brother David, who he assured the Committee would carry on everything that he (Alexander) now did. It was decided to act on this suggestion provided that David's references were satisfactory, and that he

FROM THE RWGC COLLECTION

1. Short Spoon: McEwan of Musselburgh, c. 1850. Beech head hickory shaft. **2. Baffing Spoon:** ("Baffy") McEwan of Musselburgh, c. 1850. Beech head, hickory shaft, sheepskin grip. **3. General Purpose Iron:** blacksmith made, c. 1800. Greenheart shaft, sheepskin grip. **4. Approaching Iron:** blacksmith made, c. 1800, sheepskin grip.

would accept £52 a year – a drop of 10s.0d. a week. He did, and was duly appointed, but with the title of Greenkeeper rather than Professional.

When in June 1896 he tendered his resignation it was decided that his successor should be a Professional, a player as well as a club maker – since club making must not be dissociated from the care of the green. The new man would be offered 20s.0d. a week, plus, if necessary, free coal and gas. The vacancy was advertised in *Golf* and *The Scotsman* (Scotland was still seen as an important source of golf Professionals). This time there were no fewer than fifty-five applications. Six were short-listed – J. H. Taylor of Winchester; George Lowe of Hoylake (who had applied for the post ten years earlier); J. B. Pettit; J. White; R. White; and P. Fernie. To these were added the names of Nicol Patrick, the third Patrick brother; and a Club Member made an application on behalf of a fellow Member, A. H. Molesworth, one of Royal Wimbledon's best players. The last application must have been embarrassing – it would have been difficult for most Members to adjust to the idea that their Professional was a former Member; and it seems unlikely that Molesworth had any great skill as a club maker. At any rate the successful candidate was J. H. Taylor.

He, already Open Champion, and his business partner George Cann, were interviewed on 27 June, when he was offered the job. He would receive a salary of 20s.0d. a week, a free workshop and showroom, and free coal and gas. In return he would have to be on duty at the Members' call on the three play days

5. Rut Iron: blacksmith made, c. 1750. Hickory shaft. 2-inch head to play from cart ruts. **6. Lofting Iron:** Anderson of Anstruther, c. 1875. Greenheart shaft, sheepskin grip. **7. Chole Club:** Chole was a Flanders game. One team played 3 shots towards say a barn door 12 miles distant, the opponents playing one shot away. Dual purpose, flat head combined with concave toe for lofting. **8. Putter:** Curtis of Bournemouth, c. 1908. Centre shaft, hickory, wooden head.

of each week, and keep in good condition the nine holes of the Course for which Royal Wimbledon accepted responsibility. He must also keep a stock of clubs and a staff of workmen sufficient to do all repairs. Subject to these conditions he would be free to do as he liked on the three non-play days, but he must get special leave before absenting himself for any 'out matches'. The price list for clubs which he had submitted was agreed. For a man of Taylor's reputation the salary of 20s.0d. a week was neither here nor there. He could command a fee of £10 for exhibition matches, half a dozen of which would bring in more than Royal Wimbledon were paying him in a whole year. Like others of his profession since, he wished he had been born later when the rewards were greater. But at least he had the grace to record: 'On reflection it is a churlish wish ... I should have missed the companionship of a splendid band of Professionals'.

It was not a successful appointment. Taylor admits 'My two years at Wimbledon were none too happy owing to causes that I need not explain, but the principal cause of my discontent was the restriction to three days' play a week, which put my earning power at the caprices of the weather, a factor which at all times affects the Professional's income to an extent that is rarely recognized'. There may have been other causes, but it seems clear from the Club records that restriction of earning power was by far the greatest source of discontent. Taylor was cut out to be a tournament Professional, and a showman. It quickly became obvious that looking after the Course, one of the things he had been hired to do, was of no great interest to him. In November 1897 the Green Committee had a serious talk with him, and reminded him of this particular aspect of his duties; but they accepted that as he had not been in charge very long, he must be given the benefit of the doubt.

A year later things were no better. There was now so much dissatisfaction with his performance that he was told that more of his time must be devoted 'to the care of the green'. If he refused to mend his ways Belcher would be promoted to have charge of the green men, and to keep the accounts for seed and extra labour. Instead of a Professional, a club maker would be engaged, unpaid, but with a free workshop and showroom, and the usual free coal and gas. Taylor was offered the opportunity of terminating his existing contract, and replacing it with an arrangement whereby he had the free use of the workshop and showroom which he must keep on for the repair and sale of clubs, he being free to be absent whenever he chose but receiving no salary. He accepted this proposal and, because of the greater responsibility now falling on him, Belcher's wages were increased from 25s.0d. to 30s.0d.

The new arrangement did not last long. In January 1899 Taylor gave notice he wanted to leave in March, having been offered the job of Professional at Mid-Surrey. Although he thus left under something of a cloud, he was asked back to Royal Wimbledon in 1912 to advise on proposed changes in the Course.

It was decided he should be replaced by a club maker, suggesting that Royal Wimbledon were now disenchanted with the idea of employing a tournament Professional. Willie Park (in the same mould as Taylor), Peter Paxton, R. Munro, and Peter Fernie of the London Scottish Club (the last only if his Club agreed, as Royal Wimbledon did not want to poach from their sister) were asked to make an offer for the rent of the workshop and showroom on terms which would include keeping a reasonable stock of clubs and balls, a man or men to carry out repairs expeditiously, and keeping an open shop on all play days. The prudent Park offered £10 a year, to be adjusted when the volume of business available was established by experience, Munro £26, and Paxton £52. Paxton's offer was naturally accepted and he was given exclusive rights for the sale of balls and clubs on Royal Wimbledon premises. Alas, he had bitten off more than he could chew. He had assumed when making his offer that he would employ his daughter in the shop, but the Club insisted he must engage a man, which made his costing hopelessly wrong.

Before the year was out he submitted details of his income and expenditure from 1 March to 16 October: his takings averaged £4.4s.0d. a week, his outgoings £3.12s.0d. – rent of £1 due to the Club and wages of £2.12s.0d., including those of the man he was required to employ instead of his daughter – leaving him with a mere 12s.0d. a week. It was accepted that the arrangement was far from satisfactory and should be terminated. To help him, the Club agreed to waive all rent, including arrears, until he found a new position; and they advertised in *Golf* for a Club Maker and Player.

This time the short list contained two names: R. Fullarton of St Andrews and H. Curtis of Winchester, both of whom had excellent testimonials. Fullarton was selected in December 1899, being supported by letters from R. Forgan & Son, Willie Auchterlonie, Jack White, and Mr Everard of St Andrews. He was given the usual terms, including salary of 20s.0d. a week, and the right to charge 2s.6d. a round, inclusive of a caddy should he employ one. He was told he must play only with Members of the Club, but a new development allowed him to teach ladies before 10 am and after 4.30 pm, provided his services were not required by any Member of the Club, and that the instruction was given in the vicinity of the Club premises. In June, 1902, however, he was offered a post in America, so that once again a successor had to be found.

The usual advertisements were inserted in *Golf Illustrated* and *The Scotsman*, and R. Munro, an earlier unsuccessful applicant, was selected. It was again made a condition of the appointment that he should undertake to supervise the Course, and soon after his appointment he and his assistant were asked as an experiment to look after the curling pond, although it was not part of the Golf Club. (Members of the Curling Club who were not also Members of Royal Wimbledon were given honorary membership of the Golf Club in October 1903 but this privilege was withdrawn a few months later.) Early in 1906 Munro asked permission to apply for the post of Professional and Club Maker to Raynes Park Golf Club, on the understanding he would continue to be present at Royal Wimbledon on the usual Club days (Tuesday, Thursday and Saturday) and that he would continue to keep a competent club maker there. Nothing of note seems to have occurred during his term of office, nor is it clear from the Club records why he resigned.

In the course of 1907 Roland Jones of Wimbledon Park had been employed to give advice on the layout of the new Course which Royal Wimbledon then planned; and in November of that year he was appointed Professional in place of Munro on terms he stipulated: 30s.0d. a week for 1908, with a bonus of £1 a week for 1909. At the same time Ben Sayers (Jun.) was attached to the Club. When he won the London Professional Foursomes in April 1908 Royal Wimbledon is given as his Club, as it is in the record of a match in 1908 when he beat I. Hearn of Princes, Mitcham, over 36 holes; and the fact that he was paid only £10 a year seems to confirm that he was a tournament Professional. When Jones resigned, Sayers carried on as the Club's sole Professional, and when he left in October 1912, to help in his father's factory in North Berwick, was given a testimonial. He was succeeded by Jack Fulford who remained for fourteen years – longer than any of his predecessors. As part of his contract he was allowed to have meals in the Clubhouse on special terms: plate of meat, 2 veg., bread and cheese, 1s.0d.; follow (ie a second helping): 4d.; a sweet, 2d.; cup of coffee, 2d.; tea, plate of bread and butter, 4d. (with jam, 6d.). In October 1913 he was given a week's leave of absence to compete in the French Championship. His application for an increased retaining fee was turned down, and he was given instead £10 from the Staff Christmas Fund. He was called up in 1916, when it was agreed his wife should look after the shop and that one of Messrs Forgan's employees would repair clubs. The Club continued his retainer of £1 a week to supplement his army pay of 7s.0d. He returned to Royal Wimbledon after the war, and set up a golf school, which the Committee allowed him to advertise in the Clubhouse. In 1920 his retainer was doubled to £100 a year; and almost immediately he found himself in the Magistrate's Court where he was fined for being drunk. He was warned by the Club that if he offended again the consequences would be serious. In 1922 his assistant Mickey Daragon (who later went to Tooting Bec) qualified for the final at St Andrews of a *Daily Mail* competition and a subscription list was opened to cover his expenses. There is no further reference to Fulford until February 1926 when it is recorded that he had been fined 10s.0d. for being drunk and incapable in Ridgway. He was asked to resign, having served the Club for fourteen years.

He was succeeded by Fred Leach, who remained as Professional until 1950 – ten years longer than his predecessor. In 1928 he was granted £10 towards his Open expenses, and his assistant Spen Attwood was given £2 for the Assistants' Tournament. Attwood was the better golfer, and in 1929 it was mooted that the Club should send him to the Open, but since it clashed with the Spring Meeting he was not released. Instead he was helped to play in later competitions. Leach continued to give loyal service until 1950, when the Committee felt that a younger man was needed. It was believed that a Club of the standing of Royal Wimbledon should have the services of a Professional with knowledge of the modern game, with the personality to impart that knowledge in order to raise the standard of the Members' game, and who would also be 'a high grade player'. Further, he should be in a position through his shop to supply a variety of good quality equipment at a reasonable rate from the leading manufacturing houses. Fred Leach therefore retired on pension, and was replaced. Out of a large number of applicants for the post a short list of four was selected: J. H. Busson of Formby; A. G. Matthews of Potters Bar; W. G. Branch of Berkhampstead; and Allan Dailey of Wanstead Golf Club, the last being given the appointment.

Dailey took up his duties in April 1951. He had a fine tournament record, having been fourth in the Open Championship in 1938, and a member of the Ryder Cup team in 1933. It was intended that he should devote the whole of his time to the Club except that he would be given occasional leave of absence to play in tournaments, including the Open Championship, for which his expenses would be paid. He would take charge of the caddies, being allowed a booking fee of 6d. per round or per day. In 1952, however, he accepted a post with the Berkshire. He proposed to take his staff with him, but offered to leave Nick Lyon behind if the Club wanted him. They did, and it was agreed that Lyon should remain either as assistant to the new Professional, or as a direct employee. In fact Lyon became Caddy Master in his own right, a position he has occupied ever since, ably supported by 'Mrs Nick', whose green fingers make the Clubhouse garden a perennial delight. On this occasion, instead of advertising for a replacement the Club asked the Professional Golfers'

Association to circularize their Members. Out of a short list of six the final choice fell on Russell Dailey, Allan's brother, then Professional with the East London Golf Club in South Africa. Although geography ruled out an interview, all the information about him and his war record confirmed that he was eminently suitable for the post and he was approved unanimously. He reported for duty within 24 hours of his leaving East London by air, and became the Club's longest serving Professional with nearly thirty years. He was followed in 1983 by Hugh Boyle, who played in the Ryder Cup at Houston Texas in 1967, when Great Britain lost 12–2 with 2 matches halved. In his earlier career Boyle represented Ireland in international matches and won tournaments both at home and abroad, including the Daks in 1966 and the Japanese Open in the same year.

FROM THE RWGC COLLECTION

Cut-off nose heavy iron, blacksmith made, c. 1750. Shaft 39½ inches, weight 27½ ounces.

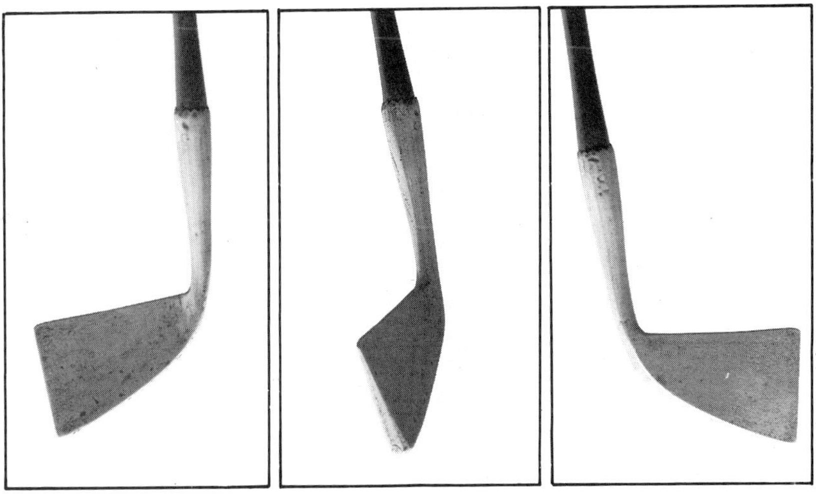

Nine

CADDIES

GOLF IS THE ONLY GAME where the player may avail himself of the professional help of an assistant, not only to carry the tools of the game, but to profer advice which may bring victory. For the club golfer in Britain, economics have diminished the influence of the caddy. He has been replaced by the trolley, carrying bag and clubs, but incapable of giving advice. In some respects the trolley scores over its live counterpart. It may safely be entrusted with the custody of a flask of whisky or brandy, which at suitable intervals during the round will provide the solace and encouragement which players in a more gracious age looked for from their human assistants; but in the era when Royal Wimbledon was founded caddies were still an integral part of the golfing scene.

Provision was made for their regulation from the start. In February 1871 the Club's second Professional, Tom Dunn (Doleman was the first), was told to see to the organization of 'the staff of caddies'. Next year an attempt was made to reduce the cost of caddying by employing boys from the National School in Camp Road, a stone's throw from the Course. The Schoolmaster, Mr J. Apperson, complained to the Conservators (responsible for good order on the Common), who said they could not help. He must write to the Golf Club. Two years later the Schoolmaster pointed out bitterly that the Golfers were still tempting boys from school in spite of the fact that the Reverend Mr Darroch (a Member of the Club) had done his best 'to check the evil' which was increasing year by year. The week before there had been an average of 36 boys absent, most of them carrying golf clubs. 'In one instance they sent a cab to take the boys off just as they were coming into school ... It is simply demoralising the school, for all want to be roaming about the Common in this idle pastime.'

The Schoolmaster confessed he had repeatedly reasoned in vain with the more respectable parents. 'The money the boys earn blinds them to their children's best interests'; and he virtuously added that he had not mentioned the reduction in the School's grant that would follow reduced attendance. This time the Conservators did intervene. They sent a copy of the letter to the Golf Club expressing disapproval.

In the next twelve months complaints about the use of schoolboys continued. The Club met them by setting up a Boys' Friendly Society, into which their wages were paid, and promising not to interfere with School attendance. When in February 1876 the men caddies withdrew their labour, the Boys' Friendly Society became part of the Club organization, the boys being classified according to competence. The more proficient were paid 1s.0d. for the long round of twenty-one holes, and 6d. for seven holes. There were regular complaints about their behaviour as they waited at the Iron House; and the Captain, J. M. Collyer, had to assure the Conservators that everything possible was being done to improve their character. For good measure the School Board Attendance Committee warned the Club that by employing boys they were liable to a fine of 40s.0d.

The Club continued to employ men after the trouble of 1876 but they were unreliable. In 1881 it was decided to use only boys. This upset the men, several of whom had caddied for years. They appealed to Tom Dunn, who told the Committee the decision 'pressed very heavily' on some who had served the Club well. Twelve vouched for by him were reinstated. A few days later supply failed to meet demand, and Dunn was instructed to recommend other suitable Wimbledon men. In 1880 grumbling by the public about the danger from golf balls led to a proposal to employ fore caddies, which was not followed up.

Meanwhile the Boys' Friendly Society, managed by George Passfield, a general factotum under the Professional, carried on. On the whole they did a good job, not universally true of boy caddies. Sir Walter Simpson, in *The Art of Golf* (1892), wrote: 'A good boy to carry is not a bad thing in its way. From him not too much must be expected. If the tees he makes are not over two inches in diameter, if each time a club is required he is not further than three minutes walk from his master, if he knows the names of the clubs, he is a good boy'.

After the move to Camp Cottage the caddies were given better facilities, including a shelter alongside the Professional's shop, which enabled the new Professional, Alexander Patrick, to keep an eye on them. In 1876 they asked to be allowed to hold a competition among themselves. A Committee Member, believing the Club had no power to stop them, gave his approval, and the Committee later added £1 to the stakes. Next year when the caddies presented 'a memorial' proposing a second competition, and soliciting a contribution towards prizes, 'it was resolved to strongly discourage the idea'; the caddies knew where their bread was buttered and abandoned the plan.

The Boys' Friendly Society was wound up, and the Club fell back on the services of men caddies. In 1889 the Captain thought their accommodation so poor that he offered to give them a new shelter out of his own pocket. The shelter was provided but in the event the Club paid for it. Next year the Green Committee was told to supervise the caddies more closely. The men disliked the new regime and over thirty signed 'a manifesto' in protest which the

Committee boldly allowed to lie on the table. Changes were made in 1892 when the caddies no longer had lunch at the Members' expense, but were given 6d. in lieu. There is no further record of protest, although even stricter control was imposed, and it seems that 'the staff of caddies' accepted defeat, although they continued to be a difficult body to manage. In October 1892 the Professional was authorized to take on a man to engage caddies on 'play days' and keep them within the yard gates. On 'off days' he would act as a Greenkeeper. This 'superintendent of caddies' (Woolgar) was given numbered metal badges for the caddies, who had to pay a deposit of 6d. – or less – at the superintendent's discretion.

Within a few months Woolgar handed in his resignation because 'the post was such an arduous one'. When the Committee employed a policeman to assist him he withdrew his resignation; but the job continued to be too much for him and he resigned finally in April 1894. The Secretary was then instructed 'to apply to the Police Office in Wimbledon for a man to take his place'.

Although the men caddies were now firmly back in the saddle, boys continued to be used, even with the blessing of the school authorities. In 1901 the Wimbledon Elementary Schools Committee resolved that no boy under 13 should be employed as a caddy, implying they countenanced hiring of boys of 13 and upwards. They even tried to encourage good behaviour in school by asking that the Caddy Master give preference to boys with a certificate of good conduct. Two years later the men blotted their copybook by writing begging letters to Members. One signing himself 'Brown' made the sensible suggestion that sober and respectable caddies should be encouraged by the Club, but it was decided that if 'Brown' were identified his services would be dispensed with. Nevertheless, a Christmas bonus, so far provided only for Clubhouse and ground staff, was approved for caddies. Those who attended regularly and were well-behaved would benefit from a special fund. In 1904 45 shared £7.6s.3d. – 3s.3d. each, leaving the Caddy Master with 1s.3d. Four years later the same number had 2s.6d. each, while three boys regularly employed had 1s.8d. Any surplus was held in reserve for those in particular need.

In 1903 at the instigation of Royal Wimbledon the Conservators took a hand in the regulation of caddies, hoping to get rid of the 'undesirable loafers' who mingled with the regulars. They asked other bodies controlling Commons 'what regulations were in force as regards the employment of caddies'. After studying the rules at Chingford Plain and Meyrick Park, they devised their own for Wimbledon Common. These were put to the Common Clubs with the explanation that they had been framed at the instigation of Royal Wimbledon to abate the growing nuisance of loafers looking for lost balls and doing serious damage.

No person was to ply for hire or solicit employment as a golf caddy without a licence from the Conservators, the licence to be subject to such regulations as might from time to time be prescribed. Further: 'Every person (other than a person actually engaged playing round one of the golf courses on the

Common, or his caddy) who shall find any golf ball on the Common shall on demand made by any Keeper or any duly appointed Servant or Agent of the Conservators forthwith deliver such ball to such Keeper, Servant, or Agent to be dealt with as the Conservators may think fit'. It is not recorded how the Conservators proposed to dispose of this treasure trove.

The regulations were comprehensive. The caddy must wear on the left arm of his outer garment a numbered badge supplied by the Conservators – his professional licence, not transferable. He must be decently clothed and strictly sober, and conduct himself in a respectful and proper manner. (It was recorded about this time that 'It is a common complaint at Wimbledon by non-golfers that the caddies are a most objectionable set, and that they appear to think that the Course is made for them and the golfers'.) He must replace turf removed by the player's club, and press it down firmly. (The first draft said 'with his feet' but these words were deleted, leaving the caddy free to employ any part of his anatomy.) The Golf Clubs must appoint caddy masters to keep a record of complaints about caddies, and to withdraw badges from those guilty of misconduct. Caddies must at all times protect the golf course and the property of the Conservators. On 1 June 1905 specimens of the caddies' badges were approved by the Conservators.

The system worked well, but there were hiccups. The Ladies' Golf Club contrived to lose the 36 badges issued to them and had to replace them at their own expense. The Common Keeper spotted members of the South London Golf Club (which the Conservators had refused to recognize, simply because there was no room for yet another Club on the Course) employing caddies wearing Wimbledon Town Club badges, and contriving to give the impression that they (the golfers) were recognized. The Conservators ordered an enquiry in which the Town Club confessed their caddy badges had been passed to the South London Club.

In 1915 the Board of Agriculture suggested to the Club that in view of the national emergency caddies over school age should be urged to register with the local Labour Exchange; and this was duly done. Two years later the Borough of Wimbledon proposed a bye-law prohibiting the employment of boys under the age of 14. Although it was open to the Club to lodge an objection with the Home Secretary, it was decided that the national interest took precedence over the needs of golfers in these difficult times – although it was pointed out that boys over 12 and under 14 could be employed with advantage to themselves on Saturdays, Sundays and holidays. When the bye-law was confirmed the Caddy Master was instructed when in doubt to get a letter from a boy's parents confirming his age. The following year the charge for regular men caddies was raised to 2s.0d. for the morning round, including lunch money, and 1s.6d. for the afternoon. Caddies not on the regular list continued to receive the old rates. In 1919 a small fund was started to tide the caddies over during a spell of bad weather when golf was impossible.

With the passage of time the lot of the caddies improved. Better accommodation was provided. The Club insured them – and their employers

– against the risks inherent in their profession – at a premium of 6d. per Member. In the 1920s a much-increased Christmas bonus was partly paid in kind. 'We used to get one pound and a pair of new boots, sir. They used to give you a chit. You got your pound, and you used to go down to the bottom of the hill, Freeman, Hardy, and Willis, to try your boots on. In them days things was so tight they pawned these boots, sir. In the end they stamped WD, War Department, on the boots so they wouldn't pawn them, that's the truth, sir.' It is doubtful whether the Club would have taken the initials of the War Department in vain. Maybe an enterprising Secretary had acquired a job lot of army surplus stores to meet the Club's Christmas liability. At any rate, in 1921 the Caddies' Christmas Fund provided boots at 25s.0d. the pair, socks, and 10s.0d. cash to every man, and 7s.6d. to each of the three boys regularly employed – and there was still a balance of £20 to be shared. When in 1924 a caddy who had been with the Club for 28 years fell sick, a subscription list was opened for him. In the same year fees were increased to 2s.6d. and 2s.0d. for men (morning and afternoon rounds respectively) and 2s.0d. and 1s.6d. for boys; and macintoshes were issued for use on the Course in bad weather.

There were pheasant and partridge on the new Course, and the Club, uninhibited by the Commons Act, which tolerated the Rifle Volunteers but discouraged the twelve bore, rented the shooting to Members. There were regular shooting parties, in which the caddies played their part. 'We went out there beating, sir. We got on the Course with big sticks and beat all the bushes and made the pheasants and whatever'd come out like, and they used to shoot 'em. And we got half a crown for that ... Some days you'd have a job going round picking acorns and chestnuts an' that for the pigs. There were pigs there at that time, sir. You'd a bushel basket, an' when that was full you'd take another. What I used to do was to make a half load of leaves and put the acorns on top.' It must be recorded with regret that some caddies practised other forms of deception. The player for whom they carried gave them a ticket at the end of the round entitling them to collect the appropriate fee. These tickets were dropped in a waste basket – from which they were occasionally retrieved to be used a second time.

There was no limit to the ingenuity of the caddies' deceptions. One hoodwinked a fellow caddy and Sir Andrew Caird, a canny Scot, by the simple device of standing behind the other caddy and thrusting out his hand to receive Caird's tip. The deception was discovered only when the rightful owner of the tip complained he had not been paid. Another, having been given 12s.0d. by Caird to replace his disintegrating boots, used the money to throw a party for his fellows at the Fox and Grapes. He was in a quandary when Caird summoned him next day to carry for him and have his new footwear inspected. The father of Bert Maddocks (See Chapter 12: *Staffs*) came to the rescue by lending his boots. When Caird pointed out they were not new, the caddy explained you could not buy new boots for 12s.0d. This left everybody happy, except Maddocks *père*, who had to cool his bootless heels in the caddies' shelter until Caird completed his round.

However, pride of place in the deception stakes must go to the five caddies guilty of the ultimate crime in golf – although it may be argued in their defence that as loyal subjects they gave great pleasure to the heir to the throne. The conspiracy – to allow the Prince of Wales in his year as Captain to believe that he had done a hole in one – had to be carefully planned. It was necessary to find a hole which His Royal Highness (handicap 12) could credibly reach from the tee in one shot, where the green could not be seen from the tee, and where the accomplice of the four caddying for the royal party could be concealed and yet see the drives – the last being essential if the Prince's ball was to be identified.

The Sixth hole at Royal Wimbledon happily meets all these criteria. It is just within reach of a 12 handicap golfer, it is masked from the tee by the majestic sweep of the rampart of Caesar's Camp, and there is ample cover in the vicinity of the green. All that the fifth caddy had to do was to wait for a day when the Prince's tee shot carried over the rampart to disappear from the royal driver's view, collect the ball, drop it in the hole, and, mission accomplished, make his escape. The plan worked perfectly. The royal party were overjoyed. The caddies received record tips, which had to be abated by one fifth to provide for their accomplice. *The Evening News* devoted headlines to the notable event.

In the 1930s the Club did its best to improve the lot of the caddies further. A fund was established to help the needy; and there was alarm and despondency when the Inland Revenue claimed it was taxable. In 1937 four-ball matches were required to employ at least one caddy, and those who did not incurred the wrath of the Committee. Caddies were given the right to play before 9 am and after 5 pm on weekdays, and at other times with the permission of the Secretary – a far cry from the days when they were denied their own competition. It was agreed they should be given new waterproof clothing, that up to £10 a year should be spent on free meals, and that if one had been sent for and not used, he should receive 6d. The Secretary was authorized to increase the number of regulars from 20 to 30. In return the caddies were expected to take more interest in the game, which meant replacing divots, and caring for the Course generally. Members were invited to report any who fell short in this respect.

The decline and fall of 'the staff of caddies' began after World War II, because of technological advance – the introduction of the mechanical caddy, referred to above, with all its limitations. In 1949 the Committee examined the Kaddy King which was offered on lease at a fixed price per round, the revenue to be equally divided between the manufacturers and the Club. After examination of the new device the manufacturer was informed that it was not practical. At this time the Chairman of the Greens Committee suggested that caddies should no longer play in the evenings and early on Saturday and Sunday. Instead five keen golfers among them should be allowed to join the recently-formed Artisan Section, so long as they continued to caddy for a minimum of 100 rounds a year. The recommendations of the National Golf Clubs' Protection Association to transfer responsibility for the engagement or employment of caddies from the Club to Members were adopted. The minimum fee was set at 2s.6d. a round. The Caddy Master was allowed to charge 2d. per round for finding a caddy and maintaining order and discipline, on condition that the Club was not liable for negligence or breach of contract.

In 1951 the services of a Caddy Master were temporarily dispensed with, it being left to the Professional to put Members in touch with caddies. However, the march of progress could not be halted. Members were taking in increasing numbers to the new-fangled trolleys. In 1954 the 'caddies canteen' run by a private individual was closed. There was still a demand for human assistance on the Course; but caddies were becoming scarcer, especially when events were held on neighbouring courses, and their fee, which had been raised to 10s.0d., now became 10s.0d. with a 2s.6d. tip. In the last three decades they have virtually disappeared from Royal Wimbledon. Two or three regulars remain, although large numbers are on call for the use of visiting societies.

Had Madame Cornuel been a golfer she would certainly have substituted for her 'No man is a hero to his valet', the more profound truth, 'No golfer is a hero to his caddy'. In the heyday of Royal Wimbledon caddies, they, like their fellows elsewhere, could suffer at the hands of their employer. One licked a ball before cleaning it, whereupon his master seized the ball, threw it away, and said: '"I don't want you to caddy for me no more." I said, "What's the cause of it." He said, "I don't know what you're suffering with. I'm not going to handle that ball." I apologized. He wouldn't have it. So I threw his clubs on the ground and walked away'. This same caddy had the temerity when carrying for a Member who did a hole in one – a genuine hole in one – to say '"That's a bottle of whisky, sir." "You don't get no bottle of whisky from me," he said. He gave me half a crown, and said "I don't want you to carry for me no more"'.

A final illustration of the relationship between master and man in the 1920s: 'I'll tell you another thing, sir. True as I sit here, sir. This is the Gospel truth. This Member used to wear black, and he had a button top of his hat, an' he had a big collie dog, that's the Gospel truth, sir. You can print this if you want to. He come on the tee, he give you a bar of Fry's chocolate, "that's for you. Now, when you see me break one of these little squares off, you do the same". I say, "very good, sir". An' this collie dog, you know, he give me twelve pieces of paper, an' he says "when the dog's done his business, you wipe his backside". An' I used to get sixpence for that. Extra.'

Some things are beyond the wit even of the electric trolley.

Ten

CLUBHOUSES

THE CLUB has had four Clubhouses. A room in Mrs Doggett's Cottage, one of several 'cottages' built into the base of the Windmill; a larger room in the London Scottish Rifle Volunteers' headquarters on the Common – 'the Iron House'; some cottages near the Eighth and Eleventh holes on the Common Course; and finally Camp Cottage in Camp Road.

An increase in membership called for something more commodious than Mrs Doggett's Cottage. A remarkable agreement was entered into – between Lord Elcho as Commanding Officer of the Rifle Volunteers, and Lord Elcho as President of the Club, which rented a room recently added to the north east end of the 'Shooting House'. The agreement provided that 'The Commanding Officer for the time being shall be President of the Golf Club, and all rules, bye-laws and arrangements shall be subject to the approval of the President'. This gave him dictatorial rights, and it became evident he intended to have his way on everything – from the largest issue down to the smallest detail of housekeeping. Thus 'Lord Elcho having expressed his views with regard to the arrangement of Club Boxes etc in the Room, it was left to the Committee of the Golf Club to carry out these views viz. that everything be arranged with neatness and uniformity'.

The Club outgrew the Iron House. In 1876 a sub-committee was appointed 'to examine various sites in the neighbourhood of the Links with a view to ascertaining their capabilities for the erection of a Golf Clubhouse'. It also considered acquiring a site from the Conservators, who at first were favourably disposed but changed their minds, and the idea of building was abandoned.

Opinion was divided about the location of the new Clubhouse. Some favoured the Wimbledon end of the Common, others the Putney. Elcho wanted something near the Iron House for the convenience of the Corps; and when Henry Lamb proposed a house near Wimbledon 'his Lordship declined to entertain it for a moment saying he wished the gentlemen present to understand distinctly that he meant to bring all his influence as Colonel of the

Regiment, President of the Club, and as a Member to bear against the removal of the Club to the Wimbledon end of the Common'.

In 1878 the Club considered taking the whole of Mrs Doggett's Cottage, if she was willing to move. Alternatively the Cottages occupied by the Professional Dunn could become a Clubhouse. The civilian element was determined the new premises should not be the exclusive property of the Corps. When Henry Lamb proposed to the Conservators taking 'the tenements now occupied by Dunn and Mrs Doggett at £60 per annum for 7, 14, or 21 years' the idea was turned down flat. 'Looking at the great demand in Wimbledon and the neighbourhood for Cottage accommodation, the Conservators are not prepared to give any of their tenants at the Windmill Cottages notice to quit, or to allow buildings for Club purposes to be erected on enclosed land in their occupation not at present built over.' The Vicar of Wimbledon may have spiked the Club's guns. He knew what was in the wind, and reminded the Conservators about the scarcity of Cottage accommodation in his parish.

At the General Meeting in June 1878, Elcho pulled out all the stops to get his way. The present Clubhouse was inconvenient. The Club had been started to induce men to join the London Scottish Regiment [was golf more popular than soldiering?] and give them something more to do than rifle shooting. They needed more room now, but since they did not want 'a St Andrews' Club or anything like that' he had drafted a plan to extend the Iron House which he had put to Sir Henry Peek, Chairman of the Conservators. Further, having heard that Prince Leopold was coming to Wimbledon to play golf, he had written to the Prince of Wales 'saying they were greatly in want of accommodation'. The Prince had replied that many of his family took a great interest in golf, and he hoped the Club would get the accommodation they so badly needed. Peek had said: 'We do not like you golfers because you come there in great numbers: you have full enjoyment of the Common and you pay nothing towards it'.

Elcho, while not accepting that the Club should have to pay, 'came to the conclusion that if anything was offered it should be a sum the Conservators would be likely to take, and which would be a bribe more or less, so that if they once took it they would be committed to the Club and so give the Club a further lien on them'. He had therefore written to Peek offering the Conservators £50 a year out of his own pocket.

Neither the wire-pulling, name-dropping, nor bribe helped. The Conservators sought Counsel's Opinion as to their power 'to erect buildings on the Common for the use of persons playing games thereon'. The advice was that they had no right to sanction an extension of the Iron House. Further, the Corps had no right to use it 'for purposes other than those of the Volunteer Rifle Corps'. Admittedly, 'if some members of the Corps, even with the association of others, were to form a private Club for cricket or golf or tennis, or any other game, and were to be allowed to leave bats, or nets, or stumps at the House it would be unreasonable for the Conservators to interfere' – but if the Iron House was substantially used for purposes other than those of a Rifle Corps they must require its removal.

Elcho, accustomed to getting his own way, was much upset. He said it had never been intended that the Wimbledon Common Act should tie the hands of the Conservators. Had he had the slightest idea this could happen he would have had the Act amended in draft, when Lord Spencer would have supported him. He now proposed to take over part of Mrs Doggett's garden, which would not 'injuriously affect her house as a residence'. The new building would greatly improve the appearance of the Common. When this came to nothing the Club looked at properties round the Common, including the disused School House at Roehampton. The matter became critical in 1880 with the notice to quit the Iron House.

In June of that year Mr Croft's cottages near the Eighth and Eleventh holes came on the market. They were near the School and the Schoolmaster feared there would be even greater pressure on his pupils to act as caddies; but the Club went ahead and rented the cottages. Town Members who had taken the train to Putney would now face the costlier journey to Wimbledon; but they saved 6d. in the cab fare. The accommodation was still less than perfect and the Club had to build its own Iron Room in the garden. Messrs Higgs & Hill put the cottages in good order and fitted them, and the Iron Room, with lockers.

The Club remained here for two years. They tried to buy the cottages, but happily the asking price was prohibitive. In April 1882 while negotiations were in progress Mr Frank Malleson offered to let his house, Camp Cottage, for 21 years. The offer was gratefully accepted, and the lease of the cottages terminated on Christmas Day 1882.

Camp Cottage was ideally situated, but much had to be done to make it a Clubhouse. The lockers installed in the cottages were removed and refitted. The 'Iron Room' was re-erected at a cost of £42.10s.0d. Today, cunningly camouflaged, it forms the Dining Room. The coach house was given a new floor downstairs, and used as the Professional's shop. The upper floor was allocated to the handyman, George Passfield and water and gas installed.

This strained the Club's finances. It was estimated that running costs would be £900, made up of £350 for rent, taxes and repairs; £75 for coal and gas; Steward, cook (his wife), and a servant, £120; the handyman, George Passfield, £52; Course maintenance, £100; Secretary's expenses, sundries, and interest, each £50; and finally, £53 for prizes, later reduced to £35. Revenue was put at £630 from subscriptions (300 Members at £2.2s.0d); 250 lockers at 10s.0d., £125; bar profit, £50; and entrance fees, £100, total £905, leaving a modest credit balance of £5. One of the more remarkable early liabilities in respect of the Clubhouse was a charge of 1s.0d. a year levied by Mrs Drax for each of three windows overlooking her estate. When in 1899 her solicitor demanded a plan of the Clubhouse in connection with the windows ('two in the WCs, and one in the room off the dining hall') he was told that if there was any further fuss about them they would be bricked up.

It is no easier to describe the evolution of Camp Cottage than it is to describe the development of the Course. In the 104 years of its existence as a Clubhouse it has grown from a comfortable six-bedroom dwelling house into a sprawling complex, as a result of innumerable additions and modifications. It resembles the handiwork of a rather stupid small boy experimenting with his first set of building bricks. It is inconvenient, consisting largely of stairs, corridors, and small rooms. The Men's Bar is so inadequate that it might have been designed by an advocate of total abstinence. The L-shaped Mixed Lounge is cunningly equipped with pillars to render inaudible remarks made by any speaker after a Club function. The Snooker Room is a morgue with a green baize slab. Rumour has it that the Ladies' quarters leave something to be desired.

It is probably the nicest Clubhouse in Britain, and woe betide any gin-palace-minded Committee that seeks to lay a finger on it.

The principal reason for the present shape, or rather lack of shape, is the presence of the large Iron Room now serving as Dining Room. Although it was added to the original Cottage, and might at one time have been subtracted with profit, it is an integral part of the complex, and it has been suggested that if it were to be removed the rest of the structure would collapse like a house of cards. Metal is cunningly hidden beneath the surface elsewhere. The lath and plaster of the Secretary's Office when drilled for the erection of shelving turned out to be solid iron.

At first only three of Camp Cottage's bedrooms were used as changing rooms, two of the others being used as bedrooms for Members. In 1883 a general post, which was to continue for the next century, began when the original dining room became the Committee Room, and another bedroom was converted to a changing room. A stray dog was adopted as a watch dog. In 1884 a plan to enlarge the Iron Room was dropped because of the cost. Next year a proposal to build a covered way from the Clubhouse proper to the Iron Room was abandoned at the instigation of Laidlaw Purves. Finance continued to be a problem, and schemes for 'extending the Clubhouse in the direction of the present drawing room, and putting two new dressing rooms over the extension, and putting a bay window in the Committee Room' were shelved. The only change immediately approved was the installation of new lockers for the increased membership.

When the owner, Mr Malleson, a very accommodating landlord, was consulted about the bay window in the Committee Room, an improvement which was to remain at the end of the lease, and an extension to the Iron Room, to be removed when the Club left, he agreed provided the window was 'substantial and ornamental'. Members may decide for themselves whether the Club carried out its obligations as to substance and ornament.

In 1893 Mr Malleson was sounded out about selling. He replied: 'I have no wish to sell Camp Cottage and do not believe that your Club will offer any sum that will induce me to change my mind, as I should find it difficult to reinvest the money in any safe investment returning the same interest.' Apparently the Club agreed with this assessment for the question of buying was not raised again until after Malleson's death. In 1925 Miss Malleson, who had inherited the property, said she wanted to sell, and the Club bought it for £6,500. (Miss Malleson must be the old lady born in Camp Cottage who visited the Club in 1975 to inspect the step ladder made by her father in 1882 by driving six inch nails into a tree by the putting green. The nails are still there but today would not support even a small child.)

The history of the Clubhouse reflects the progress of technology. In October 1885 a new boiler was installed to heat the hall by means of hot water pipes. In the same year the Committee approved the purchase of a knife cleaner and a refrigerator, in spite of the alarming cost. One of their members deputed to scour the market to find the cheapest models settled for a 6-knife cleaner at £7.10s.0d., less 12½% discount, and a refrigerator at £8.8s.6d., also less 12½%. The following year the postal authorities agreed to erect a post box in the wall of the Clubhouse front garden, where it still stands and functions efficiently 99 years later (although the garden has disappeared). In 1891 Dr Hopkinson, who lived nearby, offered to provide electricity from his own plant. Nothing came of this, and when in 1899 the question of taking electricity from the public supply was considered it was decided there was no need for it – gas was perfectly adequate. There was a speedy change of heart, however. Electricity was laid on in 1900, and 26 lights installed. There were as yet no washing machines, and there were problems with dealing with the Club's laundry. A special sub-committee was appointed because 'a great want of system having hitherto prevailed in giving out and returning the washing, and also a want of proper supervision' more methodical and economical management was called for.

There was a further advance in 1900 when the Clubhouse went on the telephone system. It had been agreed in 1899 that any Members who wanted the telephone could put it in at their own expense, it being understood that the Club would not provide anyone to attend to it; but nothing came of this. Then a five-year agreement was signed with the National Telephone Company at £17 a year. If Members made a call they were charged 3d. 'but the answers to calls made upon Members in the Clubhouse, also calls for cabs' were to be free of charge. The Steward was required to keep a record of calls. This arrangement was short-lived as the agreement was cancelled in January 1901, and in March 1902 'government estimates for applying the telephone to the Club premises' were examined by the Committee, which accepted limited service at £4 a year in preference to unlimited at £17. It was found in 1914 that telephone receipts were not satisfactory – Members were using the phone without paying for it, and a coin telephone seemed necessary.

Golf gadgets were already on the market before the turn of the century, but the Committee refused to have them in the Clubhouse. One, the Autoscout, the nature of which we can only speculate about, was offered in October 1898 by the inventor, Mr F. W. Brewster, at a rental of 1s.0d. an hour, but the Club was not interested. Mr Brewster offered to install his putting game 'Halo' in the Dining Room, but this also was properly deemed to be not quite Royal Wimbledon.

Camp Cottage, Clubhouse since 1882, incorporating the Club's earlier 'Iron Room' transferred from Wimbledon Common.

The Ladies were welcomed into the Clubhouse gradually and circumspectly. When they were first allowed to play on the new Course they changed their shoes in the building now shared by Professional and Caddy Master.

One Lady Member has recorded: 'The treatment of the Ladies in the old days was really quite laughable. When we came in from golf we couldn't even get a drink unless we were lucky enough to meet a man Member whom we knew, who would bring us one. And we had to stand outside to drink it!' The Ladies graduated into the corner of the main building. One splendid relic of those days survives – a door by the servery, invisible from the main dining room, which has two apertures – a small one through which in the 1930s the Ladies whispered their choice of meal, and a larger through which that meal was passed. It was possible for the transaction to be completed without the lady setting eyes upon, or being seen by any gentleman Member. No harem was better organized; and the fact that the door has been retained *in situ* may raise the suspicion that there is a long-term plan one day to bring it into operation again.

Finally, the Clubhouse clock. When Sir Neville Gass, a charming and well-respected Member, who had given loyal service on the Committee, died in 1966, he left his electric caddy car to the Club. The proceeds from its sale were used to provide two seats for the Course and a handsome clock which signals to anxious players on the Eighteenth tee precisely how long the principal amenities of the Nineteenth Hole remain at their disposal.

Eleven

WARS

THE IMPACT OF THE SOUTH AFRICAN WAR on running Royal Wimbledon was slight. One member of the staff – Staunton, the Caddy Superintendent – was a reservist who 'responded to the Queen's call to rejoin the army'. He was assured his place would be kept open; and he was paid the difference between his salary and army pay. The Committee considered contributing towards the equipment of local volunteers for South Africa, but found they had no power to use Club funds for the purpose. The only other hint that there was a war on is a request by several Members, anxious to have the latest news from South Africa, that the Club should take the war telegram service, but it was too costly.

It was a different story in World War I. In September 1914, almost before it had begun, the principal events of the Club year, the Autumn and Spring Meetings, the leading competitions – Silver Shield and Silver Iron – and the Club Dinners, were abandoned.

The Club's main difficulty, however, was financial. As has been mentioned above (See Chapter 6: *Members* pp. 43, 46) the war severely reduced subscription income for a variety of reasons; and the cost of everything rose year by year as the war dragged on. There was a new call on the spare resources of individual Members who remained with the Club. They were asked to contribute to a steady stream of appeals – for the British Red Cross, Princess Mary's Soldiers and Sailors Christmas Fund, the Belgian Refugee Fund, the *Daily Telegraph* Shilling Fund – the catalogue was endless.

The Club made a special effort for the Belgian refugees. Having become tenants of Warren Farm as part of the plan to acquire land for the new Course, they had spare accommodation available. £230 was collected for the unfortunate Belgians, furniture was hired to make dormitories at the Farm, and a weekly allowance of 5s.0d. for adults and 3s.6d. for children was provided for their board. At the end of the war there was still a surplus in the Refugee Fund which was handed to local hospitals.

The Club Professional, Fulford, was called up towards the end of 1916.

Barron, who had been acting as Clerk to the Secretary, was also called up at this time, being allowed £1 a week 'subject to the position he may occupy and the remuneration he may receive'. The widow of Collins, a groundsman killed in action in August 1916, was given £5. When the Greenkeeper was called up in 1918, and the question of appealing for his exemption from military service was raised, the Club decided that in no circumstances would they ask for the exemption of any employee.

An early wartime problem was insurance against damage by 'aerial craft' – a new factor in warfare, and in the daily life of a Golf Club. Miss Malleson, who had inherited Camp Cottage, showed greater foresight than the Club. She suggested they join with her in insuring against the risk; but they pooh-poohed the idea. She therefore took out her own policy for £3,000 – the value of Camp Cottage – with the Agricultural and General Insurance Cooperative Society. Later, the Club had second thoughts, belatedly recognizing that aerial warfare had come to stay and knew no boundaries, and insured the same risk with the North British and Mercantile. Miss Malleson humbly pointed out that if the Club had listened to her original proposition, or consulted her before committing themselves, confusion would have been avoided. Although the Zeppelins left the Club unmolested, the owner of the Clubhouse was entitled to feel she had scored a minor victory over the experienced businessmen who were her tenants. The Club also considered insuring against damage by Suffragettes, but decided not to.

The increased cost of living due to wartime conditions led the Club to raise their employees' wages. In March 1915 the nine ground staff on the new Course, and the two still working on the Common Course had their pay increased by 2s.0d. a week 'until the end of the war, or until further notice'. Redford, the Head Greenkeeper, the Secretary's Clerk, and the Caddy Master all had an extra 3s.0d. A year later the ground staff and the Head Greenkeeper had another rise of 2s.0d. a week; and in 1916 'in view of the increased expenses of living, it was resolved to grant a bonus of 2s.0d. per week to the green men, also Redford'. At the same time the Secretary's salary was increased to £300 a year. Early in 1918 it was resolved yet again to increase the green men's wages – to 36s.0d. a week, but only 'if necessary', which needless to say it proved to be; and in August of that year another 2s.0d. a week was authorized, this time 'if absolutely necessary'. The Steward's salary went up by £25 a year and the Greenkeeper's from 45s.0d. to 55s.0d. a week. The Caddy Master went from 33s.0d. to 38s.0d. in October 1918.

These increases, hardly astronomic by present day standards, enhanced the problems of running the Club with its restricted income. Economy was the order of the day, as the catering accounts show most graphically. It was nine months before the need for economy became painfully evident but in the summer and autumn of 1915 the most detailed costings were carried out by the Secretary in an attempt to make ends meet. Curiously enough the objective a year earlier had been to reduce prices. The fish lunch was reduced from 2s.0d. to 1s.6d.; and 'fish and a follow of cold meat' from 2s.6d. to 2s.0d. A measure of spirits had been enlarged from 12 to the bottle, or 5 to the quartern, to 10 to the bottle, or 4 to the quartern, an increase of 20% by volume. At least in the case of gin the status quo was maintained by a matching 20% increase in the price of a measure – from 5d. to 6d.; but brandy went down from 7d. to 6d.

In the first half of 1915 catering account purchases were about £100 less than in 1914, but takings dropped by £450. The utmost economy was called for, and quotations were sought from various suppliers to establish which was the cheapest. Wimbledon Model Farm, Berkshires, and Southdown Dairy all offered to supply milk at 4½d. a quart, but Calloway's (who had supplied the Club for years) won with their offer of 4d. Their quotation for best butter at 1s.5d. per lb. beat the other three by a penny. Before long they had to raise their milk price to 4½d., but when the Club sounded out the other dairies theirs had gone up to 5d. Hudson's 1s.6d. per lb. for coffee undercut Twinings by 3d., and it was decided they should be given a fair trial. The arrangement to buy soda direct from Schweppes at 1s.9d. a dozen could not be improved on: Harrods (Wholesale) 2s.8d. a dozen was hardly competitive. The increased duty on tobacco forced the Club to raise prices to Members. All tobaccos went up 2d. an ounce. Cigars also had to be increased. The British-made Club Stock No 2 went up ½d. to 3½d. each; Bucktrouts from 4d. to 4½d.; but at the top end of the range Corona Coronas were frozen at 1s.6d. Cigarettes went up 1d. for a packet of 10. To help to balance the books it was decided to charge 3d. table money on each luncheon 'as a war tax'.

The inevitable result was that catering and bar takings fell. Next year things were no better. Everything continued to go up: milk, cream, sugar, butter, and – because of increased import duty – coffee. The Club was accustomed to buying its meat from two local butchers, Higgins and Lintott, and when the former raised his prices it was decided to deal only with the latter, who had kept his at 1s.0d. per lb. (Prime joints had been 10½d. per lb. in 1913.) A tax of 8d. a gallon on mineral water led to increased prices to Members – the range including Salutaris, large bottle, 5d.; soda, 5d.; Potass, 5d. and Lithia, 3d. (both mineral waters); seltzer, 5d.; ginger ale, 6d.; and tonic, 6d. The discount allowed by the brewers on purchases of draught beer was reduced from 15% to 10%. Soap went up by 30%. The price of afternoon tea, bread, and butter had to be increased from 5d. to 6d. To reduce coal consumption a smaller and more economical grate was installed in the North Card Room, and two radiators were transferred from the South Card Room.

In 1917 the pattern was the same. Lintott increased the price of joints to 1s.2d. per lb.; but the Food Controller came to the rescue of the Club's finances by recommending that smaller helpings be served. Ale went up from 4d. to 6d. a pint, stout to 8d., Scotch from 6d. to 8d. for a large measure. Another increase in the tobacco duty put up the price of cigars, cigarettes, and pipe tobacco yet again. Coffee went up to 4d. a cup and the size of a cup of cocoa was reduced.

In the winter of 1917/1918 the Club introduced more desperate measures.

The consumption of milk was reduced from 140 pints to 70, and was further discouraged by a psychological device – the purchase of smaller milk jugs for afternoon teas. Meat consumption was reduced from 90 to 40 lb. a week, partly by a ban on second helpings. The use of margarine, which had largely replaced butter, was halved, and it was ruled that neither should be served at lunch. Cheese would be served only if specially asked for. From January 1918 the standard 1½ teaspoonfuls of tea per pot was reduced to 1. Also in January the Public Meals Order made Tuesdays and Fridays meatless days. The following month the Club dining room technically became a catering establishment under recent legislation. Whereas the staff were issued with food cards which entitled them to the meagre meat and margarine rations, no meat was to be provided for Members or their guests at lunch or dinner.

As if these progressive restrictions – which reduced dinner to something like a boiled egg and a slice of dry toast – were not enough, supplies of Scotch whisky dried up. The Secretary was urged 'to write strongly' to Messrs Findlater, Mackie & Todd (who a year or two earlier, after a careful sampling of their product, had been given the Club's seal of approval) protesting at the situation. Eventually the firm agreed to supply 3 bottles a month. Cockburn 'consented to supply 6 dozen Scotch in 1918'; but in April sales of whisky from the bar had to be suspended to give time for a working stock to be built up.

Golf Clubs throughout the country were expected to do their bit by turning over part of their land to grazing or the cultivation of crops or vegetables. Royal Wimbledon were able to make a more than average contribution in this respect by virtue of their tenancy of Warren Farm. Only a relatively small part of the farm had been used for the Course, and the balance was available for food production, and the rearing of livestock, carried on mainly by sub-tenants. Warren Farm had the ancient manorial right to graze cattle on the Common, which raised the question what size of herd might be turned loose there. The Clerk to the Conservators, perhaps surprised that there should be an enquiry about this traditional right, replied: 'I am not aware that the right to turn out cattle from Warren Farm is limited to any particular number. The right is for cattle levant and couchant on the farm, that is to say the number of cattle which can be fed in winter by the produce of the farm which can be raised during the summer'. The complexities of the formula, no doubt child's play to the medieval commoner who owned a cow or two, seem to have defeated his twentieth century successor.

In February 1915 the Town Clerk of Wimbledon wrote to the Club suggesting that any vacant land should be planted with cereals or vegetables 'to increase the supply of food for the population during the present war'; and the Green Committee was instructed to consider how much land could be set aside for the purpose. The Club had already planted two acres of a four-acre Warren Farm field with potatoes, and proposed to plant another acre shortly. The fourth acre was in such a bad state that it could not be used right away. Three quarters of an acre on the Course near the Seventeenth green (which had been intended for a turf nursery) would now be allocated to vegetables; and a small area by the Fifteenth fairway planted with potatoes.

The yield from the first potato crop was 11 tons, sold for £77, showing a profit of about £33 – having regard only to the cost of manure, preparing the land, and seed potatoes, and making no allowance for rent, rates and taxes. Mr Trustram Eve, the Controller of Cultivated Areas (War Office) was delighted with the Club's success. It was the first report he had had from a Golf Club. 'In the case of Golf Clubs I am prepared to take any amount of personal trouble, and send someone to inspect . . . In replying, perhaps you will tell me the exact position of your Golf Club – I mean geographically.'

In April 1917 the President of the Board of Agriculture made a special appeal for more help from Golf Clubs. He fully appreciated the sacrifices it would entail but he had no doubt that the Clubs would gladly make them in view of the need for the utmost effort to maintain the food supply. By this time Royal Wimbledon had eight and a half acres under cultivation, and had reached the position where it was not possible with the existing staff to maintain properly all eighteen holes of the Course and at the same time look after agricultural production. As the Board of Agriculture had asked for more hay, two plans were prepared: to convert to hay either the Second, Thirteenth, Fourteenth, Fifteenth, and Sixteenth fairways; or the Second, Fifteenth, and Sixteenth. The second alternative was chosen – not a difficult choice since it left sixteen holes available for golf (while the Second fairway would be given up, the Second green could still be played from the Fifteenth tee) compared with only thirteen holes under the former plan. In the event it was decided that the vacated land should be devoted, not to hay, but to the grazing of sheep; and it was let to the owner of Wimbledon Common Farm at £2 a week for this purpose.

Royal Wimbledon's other main contribution in World War I was the provision of hospitality to the armed forces. In July 1915 Members were allowed to bring convalescent NCOs and privates to the Club on weekday afternoons to play bowls and use the putting green, accompanied by ladies if they so wished. These guests might be given afternoon tea at the expense of the Member introducing them, but no intoxicants. A subscription list was opened to help with their entertainment. Officers from the camp on the Common were welcomed as temporary members with the right to use the Course free, except at the weekend, when they paid half the normal 5s.0d. green fee. American naval and army officers who were guests of the Pilgrims' War Club were invited to use the facilities of the Club without charge; and to show their gratitude the American Golfing Society in London presented the Club with a cup, which is still competed for – the Carr Cup, named after the then Captain. Competitions were organized to help the local hospitals. In October 1917 one which was to run for two months was designed to find the best aggregate of 4 rounds under handicap. Cards were 1s.0d. each – the proceeds to go to the hospitals – and competitors could submit as many as they chose. In 1918 the Minister of Information asked that American enlisted men on leave should have the courtesy of the Course, which was agreed except at weekends and holidays.

Finally, there was the problem that affected the whole of society in Britain – the attitude to adopt towards enemy aliens who had not been interned. This matter was raised early in the war at a meeting at the Golfers' Club, Whitehall, which the Captain of Royal Wimbledon attended, but nothing was done by the Club until June, 1918, when a notice was posted stating that the Committee 'considers it desirable that no person of German or other enemy birth or nationality, whether a naturalised British subject or not, should use the Club or Course during the continuance of the war, either as a Member or a guest'. The Rules would be changed at the next General Meeting. At this time only one Member of the Club was affected by the new rule – the constitutional validity of which may have been questionable.

The unfortunate individual was Dr Schach-Sommer, who was asked by the Secretary to prove that he was above suspicion. He put forward a defence which must have made the Committee blush. With restraint he said he had always regarded himself as a Dane by origin, having been born in Hamburg where his father was Danish Consul. Two of his uncles had fought for Denmark against Prussia and Austria in the war of 1864 – one being a Colonel of Dragoons and the other an Admiral. By annexation he had briefly become a German citizen, but had been denaturalized as soon as possible, and in 1884 became a British citizen. His nephew had won the St George's Cross and two bars in the present war fighting against the Germans and had been killed two years ago. He himself had now lived in Britain for 42 years; and had been assured by his two London Clubs that he was still an honoured member. He hoped Royal Wimbledon might take the same view. They did.

In September 1939 World War I was still fresh in the memory of senior Members of Royal Wimbledon, above all those who had played an active part in it. They were well aware of the difficulties the Club would have to surmount.

In July 1939 Miss Hutson, the Assistant Secretary (sister of a former Secretary), registered for work on the land and was given leave of absence to attend a course on tractor driving. She was later released for national service. In August the able Secretary, Captain G. N. Openshaw, was recalled for military service, the Club having agreed to make up his army pay. A replacement was found – R. A. Leppingwell. On Saturday 2 September the Club anticipated Britain's declaration of war: 'In view of the state of war now unhappily existing the Committee decided with much regret that neither the Autumn Competitions nor the Dinner will be held this year'. The pattern of World War I was being repeated; but while the Club Dinners were not resumed until after the war, modified autumn and spring meetings were held, entrance fees being devoted to charity.

A month later the Committee got down to framing regulations to meet the war situation. It was accepted that money would quickly become tight and the green fee was reduced from 10s.0d. to 5s.0d. at weekends, and from 5s.0d. to

2s.6d. during the week. Members serving with the Forces were again put on a supernumerary list. They would pay no subscriptions but on return would pay a guinea for every year of absence, and a further guinea for each month of the year in which they rejoined. On leave they would enjoy the use of the Course free. Those who moved from London would become Country Members, and any who suffered diminution of income due to the war might have their subscriptions abated. About a dozen benefited from this concession, it being understood that if they used the Course they would pay the normal green fee. Permission was granted to a resident to construct an air raid shelter on the Course where it adjoins Wool Road. Finally, sub-committees were wound up. All business would be transacted by the full General Committee.

The need for economy was recognized even more quickly than in World War I. The emergency subscription rules brought about an immediate fall in income. By May 1940 there was a net reduction in full membership of 40 (64 resignations, against 24 new Members elected); 61 became Country Members, thereby substantially reducing their contribution to Club resources; and nothing at all was received from 35 who joined the services and went on the supernumerary list.

The economy drive began modestly when in December 1939 the price of a pot of tea went up to 6d., or 8d. with bread and butter. In January 1940 'In view of the stringent economies which must be effected' it was decided that Billy, the Club horse, now 23 years old and past work, should be destroyed. There was no money for the Professional's bonus. Instead, a subscription list was opened. In March the need for economy reduced the twelve-strong ground staff to nine. The contribution to the Board of Greenkeeping Research was halved, in spite of an appeal by that body. In August 1940 the decision to waive the subscriptions of Members on active service, based on the assumption that they would be overseas most of the time had to be modified. Dunkirk had brought many of them back to Britain with the probability that they would remain there until the Second Front opened. Supernumerary Members must now pay an annual subscription of £2.2s.0d. for which they would enjoy all the amenities of the Club. Further loss of revenue followed the conversion of the Billiard Room into an air raid shelter, but the table was transferred to the Ladies' Dining Room in an effort to maintain revenue from this source.

In most respects the Club survived austerity in World War II better than in its predecessor. True, prices continued to rise – lunch to 3s.6d. in March 1941, and to 4s.6d. a year later; liqueurs from 9d. to 1s.6d.; sherry and vermouth from 9d. to 10d.; port 1s.6d. to 1s.9d.; and Bass from 1s.2d. to 1s.5d. In 1942 drinks were rationed; and £500 was invested in spirits against anticipated shortage. This prudent housekeeping avoided the dreadful nadir of 1918. In February 1944 the appalling danger that the large stock – now over £2,000 worth – might be consumed by a single bomb was so worrying that it was dispersed among several Members.

There was a progressive reduction in catering facilities, due to staffing difficulties rather than to shortage of food. In 1940 service in the Ladies' Lounge was suspended between noon and 2 pm; teas were served only in the Dining Room and on the verandah; drinks only at the bar hatch; no suppers were provided, only sandwiches, provided they were ordered before Members began their round. Service continued during air raid warnings so long as there was no immediate danger. The Acting Secretary was 'the sole arbiter of when services shall continue, or start, or stop'. Later the problems of catering became more acute. In 1944 'The number of lunches that can be served is strictly limited to, and contingent upon, the amount of food which is received, and booking before the day gives no guarantee that lunch can be obtained'. Teas would be served only between 4 pm and 5.30 pm on weekdays and until 6 pm at the weekend.

In 1945, with the end of the war in Europe in sight, Club affairs began to return to normal. The business of golf took precedence over the business of survival as a club. A scheme for affiliation with Dominion Golf Clubs of equal status was proposed and followed up vigorously. The Captain wrote to the chosen Clubs welcoming their members to Royal Wimbledon on the understanding that the courtesy would be made reciprocal. The monthly medal competition was restarted. Staffing problems diminished. Normal bar service was resumed. Repairs to the Clubhouse, which wartime restrictions had held up, and modifications to the Course were planned. The University matches were resumed. Captain Openshaw returned as Secretary on demobilization, and the temporary Secretary, R. A. Leppingwell, who had done a first-rate job, was released with reluctance.

During the war the Course suffered damage from enemy action, but the Clubhouse escaped – on one occasion narrowly, when a German bomber was brought down near the Eighteenth tee. There were six high explosive bombs. One scored a bull's eye in Caesar's Camp, on the Eleventh fairway. The others were on the left of the Fourth fairway, near the ditch (now concealed by trees); near the Tenth and Seventeenth tees; to the right of the Fifteenth fairway; and in the trees to the right of the Third fairway, near the old Twelfth green. There were two flying bombs: one right of the Seventeenth tee on the Cannizaro boundary, the other on the right of the Ninth fairway.

The last traces of wartime deprivation were swept away on Sunday 30 September 1945 when it was decided 'that after October 28th the wartime privilege as regards lunches for Ladies at weekends be withdrawn'. The Club was on an even keel again.

Twelve

STAFFS

THE CLUB has been well served by its staffs, indoor and outdoor, from the beginning.

Mrs Doggett, first in a long line, probably did no more than provide cups of tea, and perhaps wash the odd pair of socks. She was on target for immortality when a hole was named after her, but alas if you seek her name today in the score cards of the London Scottish and Wimbledon Common Golf Clubs, it will be in vain. These Clubs still play Hope Grant and Elcho but no-one plays Mother Doggett, who surely has an equal claim to the honour. Perhaps one day she will be resurrected and restored to her rightful place. For the rest of their stay on the Common, Royal Wimbledon were beholden to the less homely canteen services provided for the Rifle Volunteers.

The Aldridges were the first Stewards after the move to Camp Cottage and, contrary to the general rule, were not a success. In February 1883 'the question was raised whether it was considered that the present House Steward was ever likely to satisfactorily fill his post'. It was answered, *nem. con.*, in the negative. Tradesmen were asked to submit an account of sums owed to them, and there was a problem about missing bedding. The Aldridges were replaced by Sergeant and Mrs Cowdall, at £1 a week, out of which they had to feed a cook, whose wages of 6s.0d. a week were paid by the Club. When the Cowdalls were given a handsome Christmas present, they wrote expressing pleasure that their services were appreciated. 'We will endeavour as far as lies in our power to give satisfaction. Signed J. and A. Cowdall.' The only other staff at this time were the Booths – husband, wife, and son – who had looked after the Club's washing before Camp Cottage.

In March 1884 the Cowdalls tendered their resignations because of complaints made 'in strong language' by Colonel Lumsden (formerly President of the London Scottish Club, who had been elected to Royal Wimbledon as part of their campaign to forgive and forget). When the Steward appeared before the Committee he said that the Colonel had now apologized, and withdrew his resignation. Lumsden was reprimanded. A year later the Cowdalls again tendered their resignation, probably because there was a problem about catering profits, and this time it was accepted. It was decided the Club would now 'pay a definite salary to their servants and retain whatever profit may arise from the catering'.

When Mr and Mrs Edmund Griffiths were appointed their conditions of service were clearly set out. They would have £100 a year, with board and rooms in the Clubhouse. All profits would be for the benefit of the Club. The Steward would deal only with approved tradespeople, whose books must be made up monthly, and he would keep separate daily records of bar and food takings. He was now responsible for Booth, who had graduated to dressing-room attendant; and he had to engage a servant (paid for by the Club). The expanded membership was matched by an expanded staff. By 1894 a waiter and assistant waiter had been added. There were also two men servants paid £18 and £26 a year, each provided with two white striped jackets and waistcoats and two pairs of trousers a year.

The Griffiths resigned after the Spring Meeting in 1899, Mrs Griffiths being presented with £20 in recognition of their loyal service. An advertisement in *Golf* for a replacement produced many applicants, from whom Mr and Mrs Alfred Birt of the Castlebar Golf Club, Ealing, were appointed at £80 a year, increased within a few months to £90.

The Club's consideration for their staff is illustrated by their attitude to the Booth family. Owing to a misunderstanding Booth thought he was about to be sacked. He wrote a panic-stricken letter to every Committee Member, only to be assured that his job was secure. He may have been on the verge of a nervous breakdown, for a Club Member offered to send him on a sea voyage. He was finally given a six-weeks holiday, with financial help, while his son deputized for him. When he returned it was agreed in view of his health that he need no longer attend to the furnace. However, his health deteriorated, and after a long absence his employment was ended in March 1902, and he was allowed a gratuity of 5s.0d. a week.

The Birts, who had already had one salary increase, discovered that their predecessors had been paid £100 and asked for the same amount. When they were turned down, Birt resigned but relented at the eleventh hour, provided his increase was approved. The Committee, anxious to avoid the chore of finding replacements, gave way. In 1907 the Birts' salary was further increased to £150. In 1911 Dr Worth, a leading Member, thought Birt needed a rest. He was given 2 months' leave, and a gift of £10. The indoor staff at this time included two waiters, a casual waiter on Saturdays, cook, maid, and dressing room attendant.

Birt's poor health continued, and he resigned in 1912. The replacement – Odams – was unsatisfactory and his services were dispensed with. When Shooters' Hill Golf Club asked for a reference for him the Secretary was authorized only to give 'verbal information'. In spite of many advertisements no satisfactory candidate came forward, and in September 1914 the temporary Steward – Jenkins – was asked to carry on. Next month he and his wife were taken on permanently at £100 a year, being given ground floor sitting room, and two bedrooms, one for their child. But Jenkins did not fulfil his promise, and in January 1916 was given notice. The Secretary was instructed to find a 'Steward and Cook Housekeeper, man and wife'. They were Mr and Mrs F. W. Hurren, who had been employed at Felixstowe Golf Club for fifteen years. They had run the catering there on their own account, to the general satisfaction of the Members, but it was explained that this was not the practice at Royal Wimbledon. There were no perquisites, and no commissions or gratuities from tradesmen.

When the Hurrens retired in 1919, the Secretary's Clerk Barron, who had returned to his old job on demobilization and had helped out during Birt's illness, was offered the post of Steward, his wife 'to act as Housekeeper and make herself generally useful'. The couple proved to be by far the most successful in the history of the Club. Mrs Barron wanted to retire in June 1939 but the Captain and Vice-Captain 'were deputed to interview her and obtain her views on the matter' – in other words to persuade her to stay, which they did successfully. In spite of the difficulties the Barrons kept the Club going all through World War II. When all the staff were given a bonus in 1942 in recognition of their services under these difficult conditions, Barron sent the Committee a letter 'in which he expressed his thanks and appreciation for his recognition. Such services as he was able to render, he said, were gladly given, and in the circumstances he asked that he might return the cheque [for £50] knowing that this action would not be misunderstood'. In July 1945 it was proposed he should be made an Honorary Member. 'This was received with acclamation and passed unanimously. Mr Barron was called into the Committee Room and acquainted by the Captain of this happening. Mr Barron recorded his heartfelt gratitude.'

This unprecedented honour had to be approved by a General Meeting, and it emerged that some Members might then oppose it. Barron, being aware of the opposition, asked that the proposal be dropped. When they retired after thirty-seven years' service the Barrons received a very handsome testimonial and a volume with the signatures of those who had subscribed to it.

They were followed by the Woodlands ('Willie' Woodland had been seventeen years at Malden Golf Club) who often found the job hard going because of the difficulty of finding good staff. In appreciation of their efforts and the fact that Mrs Woodland was not in the best of health the Club financed a holiday for them in 1948. They continued to serve until March 1970. They were followed briefly by the Graftons, and in May 1972 by the Hawkins who left in 1978. Special tribute must be paid to one of the institutions of the Club, Pat Rogers, who in 1948 abandoned the profession of nursing to tend the Members of Royal Wimbledon, and whose smiling Irish eyes have for many years added savour to the massive joints she carves for Sunday lunch. Lunches have always been a feature of the Club. They received the supreme accolade on 18 February 1960 – an article in *The Times*, which included the following:

> The soup was made from stock and was not out of a tin. There followed a choice of four hot dishes, roast pork, roast chicken, steak and kidney pudding, or curried beef. Between them and the cheese came a choice of three hot puddings, and the meal served on plates too hot to handle. Beside all this a substantial cold table looked almost superfluous, the more so since the weather was cold and cheerless. The price was 6s. 6d. and the Club was Royal Wimbledon.

The quality has remained the same during the last quarter century. Alas, the price has not.

No less important for the success of a golf club are the ground staff; and here again Royal Wimbledon have been well served, especially in later years. There were problems in the beginning. Tucker, the Greenkeeper of 1884, was difficult. There was a good case for dismissing him out of hand. Although his conduct was 'very unsatisfactory in the way of sobriety and general attention to his work' the Club was reluctant to take drastic measures. 'After several resolutions and amendments had been discussed and put to the meeting, and had been either negatived or the votes equal, it was finally decided on the casting vote of the Chairman that a fortnight's notice be given him, with discretion to the Green Committee to dismiss him at any time on paying his fortnight's wages.' Tucker found a job as groundsman to a cricket club, and when it appeared there would be a three-week gap before he could take up his new appointment, the ever-generous Committee paid him a week's wages extra to tide him over.

This generosity was common form. When the 'green man' Worling, who had been with the Club many years, met with an accident at Christmas 1892, and was unable to work, he was retained on full pay until March 1893, and at a reduced rate to September 1893. It was then felt the Club could no longer be responsible, and a subscription list was opened for him. Another problem Greenkeeper was Belcher. In 1904 his work was reported to be unsatisfactory, especially when he had too much to drink. He was summoned before the Committee and given a stern warning by the Captain. In the past he had done a first class job as Caddy Superintendent, and in other positions. He was told that he was now in a key post, and if he wanted to keep it he must give up drink. Next time he drank too much he would be dismissed. 'Belcher promised amendment.' Two or three months later he was still 'taking more drink than was good for him' and it proved difficult to get good men to work under him. He was given yet another chance, this time on condition he took the pledge and never again entered a pub. Otherwise he would be dismissed. He seems to have mended his ways for some years, but in 1909 the greens on the Common Course (for which he was responsible) were so unsatisfactory that he was transferred to the new Course as second in command at a reduced wage; and he was finally dismissed in 1910.

It has been a very different story in more recent times. The Club has been blessed with 'green men' who have given long and loyal service. The Head Greenkeeper, Redford, appointed in 1923, died in 1930. He was followed by his assistant, William Cude, who looked after the Course until his retirement in 1945, with a much depleted staff during the war years. He was replaced by Sidney Stainton, 'a practical craftsman on grass, a very good organiser of labour, and first class mechanic'. Stainton, who kept bees by the putting green, retired in 1973. He was succeeded by Joe Flitton, who had joined the ground staff in 1923. Flitton served the Club for fifty-five years until his retirement in 1978, except for six years when he was serving his country in the army in India, and as a Chindit. Other members of the ground staff who spent many years with the Club were Leonard Hudson who retired in 1968 after forty-five years' service; Ranson from 1918 until his death in 1972; and Bert Maddocks, who was first associated with the Club in 1909 when he caddied as a boy, and helped in the Professional's shop. He worked in a Putney factory during World War I, returning to the Club as a Greenkeeper and later as Starter, in which capacity he was dubbed Master of Diplomacy by the Captain of 1962–63. The average length of service of these remarkable men was nearly forty years.

Bert Maddocks, one of the Club's most loyal servants: Greenkeeper, Starter, and 'Master of Diplomacy'.

Thirteen

RULES

'That's not a regular rule; you invented it just now.'
'It's the oldest rule in the book,' said the King.
'Then it ought to be Number One,' said Alice.

ALICE'S KING would have enjoyed himself on the Rules Committee of a Golf Club in the 1880s. Golfing administrators were then faced with the problem that faced the Almighty in creating the Universe; although they had longer to solve it. They too had to start from scratch. So far as the rules were concerned, their problem was in two parts. Local rules were within the jurisdiction of individual Clubs. In the case of Royal Wimbledon, as with most others, there were clearly defined areas on the boundaries of the Course which prudence dictated must be out of bounds, not so much to put a premium on accurate driving as to minimize the risk of mayhem at the fists of angry householders. If one had the misfortune to shank into Mr Smith's prize rose bed it would be foolhardy to return to the fairway by means of half a dozen slashes with a niblick. Again, the preservation of whins, to which the early Common golfers were dedicated with masochistic enthusiasm, had to be legislated for; the butts, new plantations, paths, cart ruts, and horse rides criss-crossing the Common – to say nothing of the zaribas (cattle enclosures) – all demanded special measures.

There is one early rule which seems to be capable of two interpretations. In October 1869 'Captain Page suggested that the rule enjoining 8 clubs' lengths from the hole as the maximum distance for teeing should be altered to 18, which was generally approved by the meeting'. Does this mean that there was no formal teeing ground, and that it was now agreed that the tee for the next hole should be up to 18 club lengths from the hole just completed? Or that it was generally permitted to tee on the fairway but that players had now to play the ball where it lay, if it was nearer the hole than 18 club lengths? Either way it seems an untidy rule involving a time-consuming measuring exercise.

In dealing with these matters the Club was a sovereign state. Whins were at the mercy of the local rules, subject always to the over-riding jurisdiction of the Conservators. They are dealt with in the earliest reference to rules in the Club records. In February 1872 'a player may take his ball out of the whins, and drop it behind the hazard, losing one stroke'. *May* take his ball out. If he is a soulless vandal he may expend twenty full-blooded strokes inching his ball forward, reducing the whin population of the Common by one. In June 1882 there was long discussion, in which opinion was equally divided, about the need to oblige players to lift their balls from whins 'in order to preserve the latter, as they are fast disappearing'. After more debate in July a new bye-law for their preservation was issued: 'In match play a ball in a whin must be lifted, not played ... and dropt behind the hazard with the loss of a stroke'. In medal play, however, lifting was optional: the whins had to take their chance. They continued to cause problems for the legislators: 'It should be clearly stated whether the penalty be one or two strokes for lifting a ball from whins or ravines on a Medal day'. This was now answered definitively: pick out and drop, and lose one stroke.

The early legislators need not have worried. It would gladden their hearts to see the luxuriant whin jungle between the present Eleventh and Twelfth fairways, impenetrable except at the cost of scarring for life.

While local rules had to be tailored to local circumstances, it was self-evident that the divine rules, the universal rules of golf, must be uniform. The penalty for an air shot had to be the same whether it was perpetrated at Royal Wimbledon, Royal St George's, or the Royal and Ancient; but in those distant days there was nothing to stop Clubs making it what they chose. (A Royal Wimbledon proposal to define a stroke as 'such an application of the club to the ball as moves the latter from or in its place' was withdrawn – sensibly, as it did not cover an air shot.) Individual Clubs' 'universal' rules were all very well for domestic competitions, but when a Member ventured further afield, when one from Westward Ho! came eastward to Wimbledon, unless the same rules applied, there would be confusion and irritation. Some Club had to take the initiative; and it is to the eternal credit of Royal Wimbledon that it was the first to recognize the need for uniformity.

In 1875 a sub-committee was set up to revise both the rules of the Club and the rules of the game. Their report was approved by the President of the Club, Lord Elcho, in November of that year, but alas there is no record of what he did approve. Sherlock Holmes might perhaps be able to reconstruct the new rule book from statements such as: 'The Captain was empowered to insert in Rule 13 words to clear the doubt felt by some Members whether Rule 3 applied to Medal play' – but we are no Sherlock Holmes. In 1881 another Royal Wimbledon group led by Laidlaw Purves sat down to apply their minds to the whole of the rules of golf, and came up with proposals that seemed at least to their authors to be the final answer. Two or three rules about which there was disagreement were settled in Committee.

The stage was now set for the ratification of the code so painstakingly evolved by Purves and his fellows; and it came as a considerable shock when at the General Meeting in November 1883 R. A. Deane, seconded by William

Rutherford, moved that the rules of golf as played by The Royal and Ancient Club of St Andrews should be adopted by Royal Wimbledon 'with certain bye-laws and amendments to suit the Wimbledon Green'. The Honorary Secretary, Norman Foster, was clearly upset. He said in reply that he had spent a good deal of time on the revision of the rules as recognized by Royal Wimbledon, and he challenged anybody to deny that they were the best rules of the game that had ever been drawn up. In the few particulars in which they departed from the St Andrews rules, he maintained, with all deference to that Club, that they were superior. He believed that if only they nailed their colours to the mast, Royal Wimbledon's lead would be followed by Clubs 'even as good as St Andrews'.

Laidlaw Purves thought it hardly fair that the meeting should be asked simply to adopt the rules of another Club, and so throw away years of hard work. Deane defended his proposition by pointing out that the St Andrews rules and Royal Wimbledon's as revised differed in only three instances. Under Royal Wimbledon rules a player whose ball struck himself, his caddy or his clubs lost a stroke, whereas at St Andrews he lost the hole. Striking the ball twice at Wimbledon cost a stroke, at St Andrews the hole. Under a new Wimbledon rule 'If by playing the player displace his opponent's ball, the opponent shall have the option of replacing it as nearly as possible where it lay' the Committee were proposing something foreign to all the principles of golf.

After a no doubt lively debate Deane undertook to withdraw his proposal to adopt the St Andrews rules *en bloc*, provided that the three points he had raised were put to the vote. The meeting confirmed that in the first two cases the Royal Wimbledon version should stand, but surprisingly agreed that to replace a moved ball was contrary to the principles of golf, and that the words complained of should be expunged. This was all the more surprising as it seems that Deane had not done his homework properly. St Andrews rule 36 laid down that 'if in playing, the player's ball displace the opponent's ball, the opponent shall have the option of replacing it' – almost exactly the wording Deane had bulldozed the General Meeting into removing.

Even more extraordinary is the fact that at this time there were no fewer than eleven divergences between the rules of the two Clubs – yet Deane's claim that there were only three was allowed to pass unchallenged by members who had been immersed in a study of the rules for two years. The other divergences were:

	Royal Wimbledon	**Royal and Ancient**
Ball in water	Tee behind the hazard losing one stroke	Drop, losing one stroke
Lost ball (match play)	Play another from where ball was struck, losing one stroke	Loss of hole

	Royal Wimbledon	Royal and Ancient
Lifting ball (match play)	May be lifted out of a difficulty of any description, and teed behind the hazard	Play ball where it lies or loss of hole
Loose impediments (match play)	Moving loose impediments more than a club length from the ball: loss of hole	Loss of one stroke
(medal play)	Loss of two strokes; or disqualification	Loss of one stroke
Playing opponent's ball	Loss of hole	Loss of one stroke
Ball striking player	Loss of one stroke	Loss of hole
Striking ball twice (match play)	Loss of stroke	Loss of hole
Holing out the ball	Line may be pointed out only by club shaft	Line may be pointed out but ground may not be touched by hand or club
Bad weather	No rule	Medal play may not be discontinued
Size of hole	No rule (in 1875 the Royal Wimbledon hole was a mere three inches)	Four and a quarter inches

Deane was not prepared to give up his fight for the St Andrews rules without a struggle. At the 1884 Spring General Meeting he gave notice he would raise at the Autumn General Meeting the question of the two rules on which he had been defeated. Not to be outdone, Norman Foster, who had perhaps in the meantime tumbled to the fact that there had been confusion over the rule about moving an opponent's ball, said he would raise that rule at the same time. There is unfortunately no record of the Autumn General Meeting at which battle was rejoined, and we therefore do not know how the Deane-Foster contest developed. We are indebted to *The Field*, however, for a report of the conclusion of the discussion on the rules: 'A discussion arose with reference to the want of uniformity in the rules of the game of golf, as played on different greens, and finally it was resolved that the Royal and Ancient Golf Club of St Andrews, as the premier Club, should be approached with a suggestion that they should call a conference of representatives from the various golf clubs with a view to attain such uniformity in the rules of the game, and thus remove an inconvenience which is strongly felt and which even throws doubt on the results of competitions between golfers accustomed to play on different greens'.

Royal Wimbledon, having worked hard for two years on a problem affecting all Clubs, and believing that its own code was now second to none, put its proposal for a national conference on the rules to the R and A in March 1885. The Committee must have been very disappointed at the outcome. Henry Lamb was informed by the Honorary Secretary of the R and A, Charles Stuart Grace, in a letter of 9 May 1885 that his letter 'was laid before the General Meeting of this Club on Tuesday, and that it was allowed to lie on the table'.

This pointed snub by the fountainhead to the third equal senior English Club is recorded without comment in the Royal Wimbledon Minutes. There is no reference to the fact that their immediate past Captain had won the day; but the Minutes of the Royal and Ancient reveal that the Royal Wimbledon proposal for an association of Clubs accepting a uniform code was shot down on the motion of R. A. Deane.

One consequence of the failure of the R and A to take cognizance of other Clubs' wishes for a generally accepted code of rules was that for another decade many continued to paddle their own canoes. For example, in 1891 it was still unclear how to deal with a stymie. Laidlaw Purves enquired as to the legality 'of lofting a stymie by jerking the ball over with the club lying flat on the ground'. The Royal Wimbledon Committee could not help. The matter was 'beyond their province'.

Purves wrote a long and impassioned article for *The Golfing Annual* (wearing the red coat of Royal St George's rather than that of Royal Wimbledon) making the case for uniform legislation. One target of his criticism is reprimanded for claiming that most Scottish Courses were Commons never under the plough, and did not need rules 'about balls driven into men's gardens and whatnot'. 'May I ask, in passing, how this applies to the three greens of Scotland on which there is probably more play than on all the other golfing greens in Scotland together viz., St Andrew's with its rig and furrow land, its Swilcan burn, Eden, and sea, its station-master's garden, and its seats; North Berwick, with its plantations, quarry, well, gardens, and stone walls; and Musselburgh, with its posts and rails, walls, macadamised road, windows, and Mrs Forman's garden.'

Purves said he did not contend for the superior excellence of the English codes over the Scottish (as a Scot he would hardly do that) or the code of one Club over that of another. 'What I do maintain is that these so-called innovations in the English codes are often worthy of consideration, and that the upholders of the St Andrews code of 1882 in opposition to the proposition for a golf legislature have supported their contention by statements which are misleading and inaccurate ...' He poured scorn on one advocate of the St Andrews 'sacred book' who claimed that a hazard from which a player could not escape in two strokes called for 'the interference of the Greenkeeper', while he accepted 'a defunct sheep or other malodorous object' as a rub of the green even on the putting surface. Golfers who wanted a central legislative body 'do not care much what rules St Andrews may find necessary to evolve as to clothes, or washing tubs, or gardens, or whins, or other eccentricities of that sort'. What they do want are rules to cover situations common to all Courses. Therefore the views of the many Clubs disagreeing with St Andrews should be examined dispassionately 'and not in the facetious and jocular method in which some critics of the proposal have thought fit to indulge'.

Willie Park Junior had some sympathy with this assessment. In *The Game of Golf* (1896 edn) he wrote: 'It is somewhat unfortunate, however, that the rules which they [the R and A] have framed are not sufficiently comprehensive ... it would almost seem as if they had been drawn up with reference to the St Andrews Links alone'. They did not apply generally – exactly Purves's point. 'The only other Club which has framed a set of rules for itself is the Royal Wimbledon Golf Club; but I am not aware that their rules are adopted by another Club in preference to the St Andrews' code; and such a proceeding in Scotland would be deemed little short of sacrilege.' Park considered that both sets of rules had their good and bad points, but no doubt because St Andrews was St Andrews, he preferred the R and A's.

In one case Royal Wimbledon did go off the rails. In 1894 the Committee decided by a majority of 6 to 4 that a ball on the wrong putting green should be dropped without penalty not nearer the hole being played 'except on Medal Days when the ball must be played where it lies'. There is no record when this horrific piece of legislation was repealed.

It was not until 1896 that Royal Wimbledon's attempt to bring uniformity into the game was followed up. The Secretary of the Delegates to the Amateur Championship proposed a meeting to discuss the formation of a Golf Union, which among other things would have ensured uniform rules. The Captain of the R and A, briefed to frustrate the attempt to set up a competing body, succeeded; but a letter from Royal St George's suggesting a Rules Committee led to a meeting of leading Clubs, other than the R and A, which drafted a constitution for a Rules Committee. This the R and A rejected in May 1897 by 64 votes to 61, and later that year decided to set up its own Rules Committee. This made possible the uniformity for which Royal Wimbledon had been campaigning for so long, and in April 1898 a General Meeting of the Club voted overwhelmingly for the adoption of the St Andrews rules.

Fourteen

COMPETITIONS

COMPETITIONS make a golf club a Club, as distinct from an aggregation of individuals ploughing lone divot holes. It would be interesting to know when the first took place. No-one sat down to invent a game calling for club, ball, tee, fairway, green, hole, and a minimum of two players. More likely the kilted North Britons alluded to earlier found that hitting stones quickly palled. Had not someone boasted he could do it better, there would be no golf today. We owe all to the competitive spirit.

The pattern of competitions has been uniform since the game began to be played in earnest in the 1870s, one reason being that leading players belonged to several Clubs, so that there was cross-fertilization. Most Clubs have had a monthly medal and spring and autumn meetings from the very beginning, supplemented by knock-out competitions held during the year, and competitions for cups presented by Members. Royal Wimbledon has not deviated from the general pattern.

The monthly medal was well established on the Common Course by 1869. (The first recorded medal was in November 1867 – see page 11.) In May 1869 the medal, played over 3 rounds of the seven-hole Course, was won by Mr Fowlie, with 112 – an average of 5.3 a hole. Mr D. Lamb was second with 114, Mr C. Lamb third with 122, and Lieutenant Porteous fourth with 126. It is recorded sadly that 'the other players gave up' except Mr Baillie, who struggled round in a fraction under sevens. The winner was awarded the Medal and 12 balls, the second 6, the third 4, and the fourth 2. Henry Lamb, elected in November 1869, won the December 1869 and January 1870 Medals played over fourteen holes, in 70 and 77 respectively. In April 1871 the medal was played 'over one long round 18 holes and one short round 7 holes – 25 holes in all' in high wind. Messrs Fowlie and Smith tied with 132 and Smith won the play-off by 5 strokes over a short round.

At first all played off scratch – the earliest reference to handicaps is for the April Medal in 1871. It was still a scratch competition, but 'a Pewter presented by Mr Usher was played for at the same time, the Players being handicapped', with a limit of 24. Messrs Smith and Fowlie tied with 132 gross playing off scratch. Smith won the play-off over a short round by 5 shots, taking both Medal and 'Pewter'. The Reverend Mr Darroch came third in the Pewter with 148 less 12. There were handicap competitions in the Spring Meeting in 1873, but it was not until February 1874 that the medal was played for on handicap. 'On Saturday the 28th inst., and in future, players competing for the monthly medal will be handicapped – odds being given up to 18 strokes in the round of 18 holes.' Next year the Secretary was authorized to consult the Professional Dunn about the handicaps of Members unknown to the Committee 'and to alter them should Mr Dunn's reasons for doing so appear to him to be well founded'.

Winners now received a miniature medal with ribbon according to handicap on a sliding scale:

Scratch, medal with star of	10 rays
Any odds up to 4,	8 rays
5– 8,	6 rays
9–12,	5 rays
13–18,	4 rays

The early medals were popular events, fully reported in the press. In February 1878 Mr F. G. Faithfull's net 106 won 'the Medal and Memento Star of 5th Class' – with a mere 4 rays as his handicap was 18. Forty-four players had entered, their gross scores ranging from Mr R. A. Deane's 93 (off scratch) to Lord Ruthven's 122. In the following year the medal had to be cancelled in January and February because the Course was deep in snow, but play was possible in March, when 'There was a good muster of players; but there was also a rather strong wind blowing ... and this was doubtless the cause of a number of them suppressing their names and scores at the completion of the round, and of others, more modest still, scattering the torn fragments of their scoring cards among the whins at an earlier stage of the proceedings. Some there were, however, who had the pluck to hand in their cards with heavy totals, thinking it only fair towards the winner ... that they should swell his triumph'. *Plus ça change, plus c'est la même chose* –

The Spring and Autumn Meetings naturally attracted bigger entries. There were 67 competitors on the final day of the Spring meeting in 1878. The Meetings were highly-ceremonial three-day events with generous prizes, provided by the Club and by individual Members. In the early days the main annual competition was the Challenge Medal; but in 1873 a full scale Spring Meeting was held on 19, 22, and 23 April when prizes presented by Members included a silver Claret Jug, 'a set of Prize Clubs', and a pair of silver Dram Flasks. When Mr H. M. Strachan, not a member of the Club, presented a challenge Silver Cup, the Committee unanimously elected him a Life Member. The Annual Challenge Medal went to the player with the best scratch score; but there were also prizes for the five best handicap scores: sets of clubs value £2.2s.0d., £1.10s.0d., and £1; a dozen balls (15s.0d.); and 2 clubs (10s.0d.).

On the second day the Claret Jug and a set of clubs were competed for on handicap; and on the third, also on handicap, Mr Strachan's Cup and Past Captain Usher's Dram Flasks – one round, Members having to nominate the prize they played for. Some thought the Committee were too generous with prize money. In 1875 £20 (say £500 at today's prices) was provided (the conversion factor of 25:1 is roughly confirmed by two key commodities. In 1875 a golf ball cost 1s.3d., and a dram 2d.). When this went up to £30 two years later there was murmured protest and Committee Members were asked to sign a statement declaring they approved the increase.

Competitions – and indeed the game in general – were taken very seriously in the last decades of the nineteenth century. After the Autumn Meeting of 1874 Henry Lamb protested that in the Strachan Cup Competition no player should have received more than 18 strokes which meant he had tied for first prize. He was told there was no such rule; and further, he was invited to justify an allegation that handicaps were changed in mid-competition. It turned out that Mr A. G. Mackenzie had begun the three day meeting on 20, which was reduced to 18 by a single member of the Committee. It should have been a Committee decision; and in any case it was wrong to change a handicap during a meeting. 'I request that you will allow me the full number of 20 which was given to me by those entitled to do so, and adjudge the prize to me.' The episode led to a spate of resolutions. Finally, the aggrieved Mackenzie was instructed to play for the 3rd, 4th, and 5th prizes against Lamb and Laidlaw Purves, the others in contention.

The handicap limit for the Monthly Medal was now fixed at 18, individual handicaps being left to the Captain and Secretary. 'No Member shall have the right to question their decision.' Spring and Autumn competitions would be played with unlimited handicaps, unless the donor of a prize determined otherwise.

The seriousness with which all concerned treated competitions is illustrated in May 1875 when 'A question having been submitted to the Committee of the Club with reference to J. C. Fowlie's score for the May Medal, the Honorary Secretary was requested to ask Fowlie and George Gosset to state the circumstance in writing which led to the opinion of the Committee being asked'. Whereupon Gosset (whose father founded Westward Ho!) made a statement in which Fowlie concurred: 'At the third hole Fowlie, having played two strokes, lay about four feet from the hole; the third stroke missed, and he lay about six inches on the other side. Fowlie, being riled, struck the ball with the back of the club, and failed to hole, picking his ball up which lay about four inches from the hole. Not being quite sure about the rule, I persuaded him to drop the ball over his shoulder'. The Committee were unanimous in their decision. Mr Fowlie was disqualified from taking any prize in the competition, 'he having when competing lifted his ball unnecessarily on a putting green when within four inches of the hole'. George Molesworth was declared winner of the medal.

The causes of the principal dispute of 1877 are shrouded in mystery. A complaint was lodged in March by John Blackburn and Donald Campbell against Messrs W. Steven (a Committee Member), J. Steven, I. Aitchison, and H. P. Cumming. Written statements were read, and the parties were asked to make 'a fuller and more minute statement of their complaint'. In May the dispute was still before the Committee; and a Minute by the Captain was sent to both sides ... At the next Committee Meeting John Grant (who was not involved in the original row) took exception to the Minute, and 'making his protest against that part of it which referred to the Tenth hole, resigned his place on the Committee, at the same time leaving the room'.

This must have been a particularly weighty case, for Aitchison, Cumming and the Stevens appealed to Lord Elcho five months later. When the Captain reported the results of an interview with Elcho, the Committee unanimously reaffirmed their earlier decision – whatever that was. 'But it was agreed that according to His Lordship's suggestion explanations of the expressions used by Mr James Steven, which were considered censurable, might be tendered through the Committee as his apology.' What did happen at the Tenth hole to arouse such passion? Did the two-ball drive into the foursome? Was it something more sinister? We shall never know as the records, at one time so faithfully kept, have perished.

On the last Saturday of November 1890, Monthly Medal day, deep snow did not deter A. H. Molesworth, the most ardent competitor (dare one say pothunter?) of the era, and one other from fighting their way round – a seemingly impossible feat. Molesworth's handicap had just gone from scratch to plus 3 because of his gross 76 in the previous Autumn Meeting, when he won the Steven Challenge Cup, the Club Gold Medal, the Anderson Beakers, the Davidson Medal, the Handicap and Scratch Aggregate Tankards, and perhaps the cordial hatred of his fellow competitors. (In reporting his successes *The Field* speculated as to just what the Handicapping Committee would do to him.) On this occasion he was round in a gross 106, his partner in net 120 (140 less 20) so yet another pot went to Molesworth. The indefatigable Dr Purves had a year or two earlier raised the question of snow rules, when it was decided that 'The ball must be played as it lies, or may be lifted and dropped, losing a stroke, after preparing a place to drop in'. The foregoing figures suggest that Molesworth had approximately 30 penalty strokes, and that his unfortunate caddy may have suffered from frostbite after clearing 30 dropping zones for his master.

A few years later Molesworth's will to win was not impaired. When his partner penalized him 2 strokes for grounding his club in a whin and he appealed against the penalty, he was told 'it was a universal custom in Wimbledon not to ground one's club in a whin' and that the penalty stood. A further appeal was no more successful. In 1900 he was involved in a dispute over a round in the Silver Shield Competition, and again the Committee ruled against him.

The variety of objection and appeal in these early days is unlimited. When Mr George Muir won the Monthly Medal in January 1888 the runner-up immediately protested that he had not paid his subscription. Muir countered with an elaborate defence. Admittedly he was in arrear, but this did not debar him from the competition since under Rule XI his name would not be posted until 1 February, up to which date public opinion did not deem him to be in arrear. However, if the Committee ruled against him his entry was void *ab initio*, and he begged leave to withdraw his card of score, and particularly to request that he be not published in the newspapers as a competitor. 'To such publication I have the most decided objection.' The Committee decided he was technically in arrear and forfeited the Medal. When Edgar Wight won the Bombay Cup in 1898 he seems to have been prompted by Dr Laidlaw Purves (who had a finger in every competition pie) to have misgivings. The Committee listened to Purves for over an hour, and later discussed the matter with Wight for an hour and a half. At the end of the day the Committee resolved: 'that Mr Wight had honourably won the Bombay Cup, but that he would have done more wisely had he informed the Committee that he had the previous week won a prize at Worcester with a very low score'. Purves agreed to withdraw a certain letter, and then Mr Wight agreed to withdraw all his charges, and that the correspondence should be destroyed.

In 1897 I. M. Kerr entered a Competition on his Royal Wimbledon handicap of 9, when he was 8 at Sandwich and 5 at Beckenham 'which facts he had omitted to communicate to the Secretary according to the rule passed at the last Autumn General Meeting'. His attention was drawn to the omission and his opponent declared the winner.

Nothing was too much trouble for the early Committees. When Dr Walker, while playing in the Monthly Medal in March 1900, had the misfortune to drive into a post hole that had not been filled in, which cost him two shots and the Medal, he naturally lodged an appeal. Before giving judgement several members of the Committee visited the scene of the unfortunate occurrence, and after due deliberation deemed the hole ground under repair, and gave the deprived doctor the Medal.

The Monthly Medal is the Club's oldest competition, but the most venerable are the Silver Iron and the Silver Shield.

The 'Silver Iron with ebony handle' was presented by William Porteous in November 1882 for a foursomes knock-out competition. He hoped it would 'relieve the pressure on the green by encouraging foursomes play, and bring players of different calibres together, and mix the men. The natural tendency is gradually to get into the habit of playing against the same opponent day after day in a single'. At first if a match was all square after eighteen holes, a second eighteen were played, but in 1885 it was decided that 'the competitors shall continue to play hole by hole till the winning couple is determined'. In 1882 it was won by the Crawford brothers, donors of the ceremonial Silver Club, who 'irresistably shouldered their way through all the heats, showing that at golf too the boxing axiom "weight must tell" at all events sometimes holds good'.

The Silver Iron produced the usual quota of squabbles. In 1888 Messrs

The Club Gold Medal, presented in 1873 by James Lindsay Bennet, now awarded to the scratch winner in the Autumn Meeting, Second Saturday.

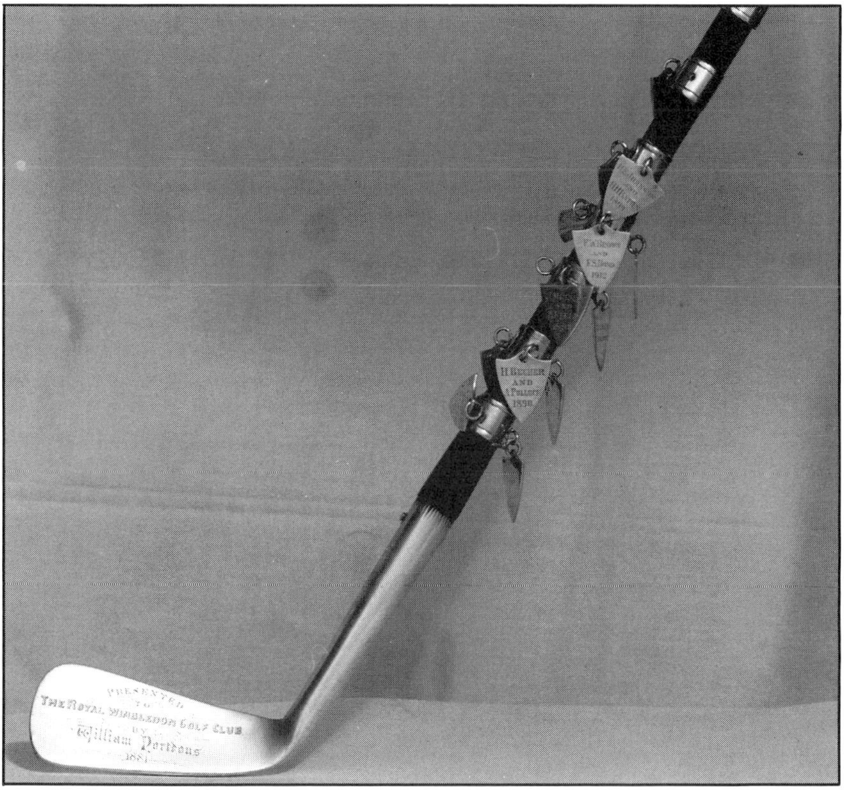

Silver Iron 'with ebony handle' presented in 1881 by William Porteous (Captain, 1872-74) for an annual foursomes knockout competition.

Lamb and Skene protested against their defeat by Messrs Cameron and Ridpath. Lamb, an interested party, withdrew from the Committee Meeting 'and after reading various letters on the subject from the Members concerned it was decided Messrs Cameron and Ridpath's names should be inserted as the winners'. Mr Taylor complained that his partner's handicap had been changed (presumably downwards) after the draw for the Silver Iron; but the Committee saw no reason to overrule the Handicapping Committee.

In 1886 Alexander and David Davidson presented a Challenge Shield for a knockout singles tournament, and a £10 prize for the first three years: 'the odds to be two-thirds of the difference between the handicaps of the two opponents in each match'. The handicap formula for the Silver Iron foursomes was 'one-third of the difference between the aggregate handicaps of the players as coupled'; but experience suggested that these formulae were weighted against the higher handicap players. In 1888 they were changed by Lamb and Purves to three-quarters of the difference for singles and three-eighths of the partners' combined handicaps for foursomes. The problem posed by fractions of a stroke produced by the formulae, which originally had been ignored, was now legislated for: 'where half occurred it should count as one'. This is one Royal Wimbledon initiative that has universal acceptance at the present time.

In the early days it was not unusual for a tied match to be settled – hopefully – over a second eighteen holes. In 1905 the Committee helped those with less than average stamina by ruling that 'in the case of a tie at the Eighteenth hole, three additional holes shall be played, and if the match is then still undecided, the competitors shall play hole by hole until the match is decided'. Later, competitors were allowed to agree to some other arrangement for settling the tie at the Eighteenth, including no doubt the toss of a coin.

The creation of two Clubs out of the London Scottish raised a problem – what to do about trophies, of which the principal was the Hope Grant and Elcho Medal, donated by General Sir Hope Grant and Lord Elcho, and first won by Private Cheyne in 1868. Elcho wrote unpleasant letters demanding the return of the medal. Colonel Moncrieff, ever a statesman, said he had no wish to comment on their tone; but thought that as Elcho claimed the medal as surviving donor, it must be returned. This was approved unanimously. Guy Pym said he understood the monthly medal had been paid for out of the funds of the Rifle Corps, and that it must also be returned. Mr Stephen Smith presented 'a handsome medal for monthly handicap competition' to replace that surrendered to the Corps.

It would no doubt have gladdened the hearts of the early donors of trophies, and perhaps astonished them, had they known their trophies would still be competed for far into the next century. The Bennet Gold Medal dates from October 1873 – 'a Gold Challenge Medal presented by James Lindsay Bennet Esq., to be played for annually at the Autumn Meeting'. It was unanimously resolved to elect Mr Bennet a Life Member 'as the Committee is informed that the Medal is both intrinsically and as a piece of art of much value . . .'. It is still

Silver Punch Bowl, presented in 1888 by J. L. Ridpath (Captain, 1887-88): Spring Meeting, Handicap limit 10.

awarded to the scratch winner on the second Saturday of the Autumn Meeting. When the Royal Bombay Golf Club presented the Bombay Challenge Cup (as part of an exchange of trophies with Royal Wimbledon) in the Spring of 1877 it was understood it would be played for under handicap at the Spring Meeting, and it is still the handicap prize at that Meeting. The winner of the Autumn Handicap is awarded the Steven Challenge Cup, presented by the Captain of the Club, William Steven, in November 1876 'to be played for under handicap annually at the Autumn Meeting, the winner to hold it for a year'. In 1888 J. L. Ridpath presented 'a very handsome old silver punch bowl to be played for at the Spring Meeting with a 9 handicap limit'. He accepted that the limit 'will deter many players ... which I shall regret, but on the other hand I feel a Captain's prize should be given to encourage good golf'. The Ridpath Bowl is still played for at the Spring Meeting, handicap limit now 10.

When Henry Lamb presented a medal in 1887 he laid down elaborate conditions: '(a) the Medal to be "The Champion Medal of the Royal Wimbledon Golf Club" and the winner the Club Champion for the following year; (b) to be won by the player who makes the most best scratch scores in Club stroke competitions between the Autumn and Spring Competitions; (c) each win during that period to score One – if two men tie each to score ½, and if three tie ⅓ and so on; (d) if two or more tie at the end of the year, the winner to be decided by adding together the scores made in competitions in which both or all played; (e) the Medal to become the property of the winner each year; and (f) the Committee to reserve power to alter the above conditions'.

Silver Shield, presented in 1886 by Alexander and David Davidson for an annual singles knockout competition.

The Colombo Elephant, presented in 1953 by the Royal Colombo Golf Club: aggregate Handicap, Autumn Meeting.

Bombay Challenge Cup, presented by the Bombay Golf Club in 1876, played for under Handicap at the Spring Meeting.

The Ladies' Scratch Cup, first won in 1891 by Lena Thomson, Captain, 1893, and English Ladies' Champion, 1898.

Lamb showed typical commonsense in adding the last condition since his formula called for a computer. His Medal is now awarded for the best scratch aggregate for the four rounds of the Spring and Autumn Meetings – near enough to what he intended.

The Spring Meeting of 1892 included a long-driving competition on the Saturday evening, which reveals the potential of the heavy clubs and gutta balls of the time – 'the promoter and prize-giver being Mr John Murray, who offered a beautiful silver coffee-pot for the longest drive, the carry of the ball only to count, each competitor to have 3 drives'. Twenty Members competed 'in a light air of wind, which although across the Course, was favourable ... Permission had been kindly granted to use the field behind the Clubhouse, so ample and unrestricted space was available, allowing careful marking and timing of the balls'. The four longest drives were:

	Handicap	*Yards*	*Feet*	*Inches*	*Time*
The Hon. Ivo Bligh	8	185	2	6	5½ secs.
Mr J. E. Faithfull	3	182	1	5	6 secs.
Mr F. J. Walker	5	178	–	–	5½ secs.
Mr H. S. Colt	Scratch	173	–	–	5¾ secs.

'Dinner in the evening at the Clubhouse terminated the day's pleasures, of which it was not the least; songs, sentiments, speeches, and recitations coming willingly at the Captain's call.'

Competitions more recently instituted which are popular with Members and The Higgins Trophy, a Challenge Cup presented in 1923 by William Higgins to be competed for 'by veteran golfers of 55 and over'; and the more recent Nicholson Veterans' Cup, no doubt inspired by the increasing longevity of the membership, which deems that veteranhood begins at 65. The Millard Weight for Age Cup for the lowest net score less the competitor's age, which gives centenarians a good chance of a trophy, is also popular. The Ellis Cup, a knockout Mixed Foursome Competition, is the principal event in which the sexes rub shoulders on the Course, but a recent innovation in the summer – a series of Ten-hole Evening Foursomes followed by supper in the Clubhouse – with a prize donated by Graham Barber, son of a former Captain, provides another opportunity for the sexes to recognize each other. Another recent innovation is an informal Vocational Competition held in May, when professional teams – Technocrats, Bureaucrats, Adjudicates (in 1986 four High Court Judges, led by the Captain), Numerates, Medicates, etc., but no Golfers – compete with each other for a free lunch.

Trophies originally won by Mr G. E. Grant Govan, and his son, an airman killed in World War II, were recently returned to the Club by his daughter. They are now played for in a revived Men's Winter Foursomes Competition which lapsed some years ago.

Three competitions outside the Spring and Autumn Meetings must be mentioned. The Carr Cup, presented to the Club by American Officers in gratitude for the courtesy of the Course in World War I. It is named after

Arthur Carr, Captain in 1916–1918, and is played for in June (medal); the Witts Cup (August Stableford, originally won as Captain's Prize by A. C. Witts in 1926, and presented by his son Derek for an annual competition); and the Guy Johnson Trophy presented in 1947 by Henry Johnson in memory of his brother who was killed in World War II. Finally, there are the very popular Monday afternoon four balls, instituted by the late Alex Hendry, a Past Captain, in which partners and opponents are found by drawing playing cards. Fourteen holes are played, the losers' liability being limited to the provision of afternoon tea, sometimes, in the case of more exacting victors, including jam.

The Course record of 67 by J. A. Simmonds stood for thirty years until it was broken by Joe Connolly (handicap 5) in the August Monthly Medal in 1979 with gross 66. His card read as follows:

Hole	*Yards*	*Par*	*Score*		*Hole*	*Yards*	*Par*	*Score*	
1	405	4	5		10	476	5	4	
2	426	4	3		11	421	4	3	
3	382	4	4		12	455	4	4	
4	401	4	4		13	161	3	3	
5	164	3	4		14	455	5	3	
6	261	4	3		15	421	5	5	
7	500	5	3		16	390	4	5	
8	221	3	3		17	138	3	3	
9	282	4	4	33	18	341	4	3	33
									Total 66

Club Members have distinguished themselves in national competitions from the earliest days. Those who won at the Royal and Ancient include Henry Lamb – the Gold Medal in 1873 and 1878, and the Silver Cross in 1871 and 1873; and Roger Wethered – the Gold Medal in 1921, 1923, and 1937, and the Silver Cross in 1934. The Queen Victoria Jubilee vase was won by Harry Colt (who redesigned the Royal Wimbledon Course in 1924, and was a member of the original R and A Rules Committee) in 1891 and 1893; by V. A. Pollock in 1907 and 1927; and by A. V. Bridgeland in 1952. One of Henry Lamb's greatest successes was his defeat of the redoubtable John Ball Jr (Open Champion in 1891) by 6 and 5 in the semi-final of the first formal Amateur Championship in 1896. (An amateur competition at Hoylake in 1890 had been such a success that the winner – A. F. Macfie – was deemed to be the first Amateur Champion.) Lamb was defeated in the final by Balfour Melville. Sir John Cradock-Hartopp reached the semi-final of the English Championship in 1935, and Arnold Bentley won it at Birkdale in 1939. Royal Wimbledon has another important link with the Championship, being one of the seven Clubs that originally sponsored it, a fact recorded on the Trophy.

John Bevan, one of the Club's youngest Captains (1983–84), played for Wales in 1964–67, was non-playing Captain of his country in 1972, and playing Captain in 1973–74. Robin Rutherford played for Scotland in 1938 and 1946, in which years he was runner-up in the Scottish Amateur

Championship. Roger Wethered, who won the Amateur Championship in 1923, represented England every year from 1922 to 1930, and Great Britain in the Walker Cup in 1921–23, 1926, 1930, and 1934.

The last's legendary failure to win the Open Championship at St Andrews in 1921 – surely the greatest hard luck story in golfing history – must be recorded, if only to correct apocryphal versions. After going forward to study his second shot at the long par 5 Fourteenth hole in the third round, he walked back and accidentally touched the ball with his heel, a one-shot penalty. He put his next shot on the green, one of the few competitors to do so, and got his par. In the final round he played a near perfect shot to the Eighteenth, where the pin was near the front of the green, and got a bad bounce. The ball rolled back into the Valley of Sin, and he took 3 more to get down. Fortune which thus frowned on the amateur, smiled on his nearest rival, the Professional Jock Hutchinson who earlier had a hole in one which enabled him to tie after 72 holes. Wethered was due to play in a cricket match next day and was reluctant to leave his side in the lurch. He was prevailed on to put the Open Championship first. In the 36-hole play off Hutchinson won by 9 shots.

In 1939 Royal Wimbledon instituted a team putting competition on their splendid green (which Henry Longhurst described as the best of its kind, and of which Bernard Darwin wrote 'The Wimbledon putting course seems to me, if I may respectfully say so, a model of what such a course should be. It occupies an acre; it is a miracle of velvety smoothness; and though it is full of subtle and interesting borrows, it is not in the least fantastic'). Twenty-four Clubs sent teams of four in June which competed in groups, the winners playing off against each other. The competition was resumed after the war, and has been held annually ever since. Now thirty-two teams of four, including many old boys' teams, take part. Eight compete each evening for four days, and the four winning teams and four runners-up play each other on the final day.

'Finally, I observed one pleasant custom, namely that after each match the combatants retired to the open-air bar in the verandah, where they cordially pledged one another. I asked a very important person in the Club whether as the evening wore on the putting in general improved or otherwise. He said it became unquestionably bolder and better. Whether or not he was right, this was a most cheerful doctrine befitting so thoroughly cheerful a competition.' Thus Bernard Darwin in 1952.

Fifteen

MATCHES

THE FIRST RECORD of an inter-club match is in 1867, (in the fragment of the earliest Minute Book in the possession of the London Scottish Golf Club). It was arranged to play Blackheath on Saturday 7 December. There is however no record of that match in the Royal Wimbledon papers, nor of a return match in the following year; but the Royal Blackheath Club were guests at Wimbledon on 'a cold showery day' in April 1869 to play a 14-a-side singles match 'man against man. Three rounds of the ground = 21 holes. To count holes, not strokes'. When it was proposed that a tent should be hired to accommodate the teams at a cost of £2.10s.0d. Mr Mackenzie pointed out that the Club had no right to use its funds for this purpose, and it was agreed the team (which was selected by the votes of the Committee) should foot the bill. Blackheath won 10-3, with one halved, or by the method of scoring then used by 38 holes to 8, the score at the end of the round being counted. Lord Elcho, playing second for the Wimbledon side was 3 up, one of the two winners for the home team. 'The Members of the Royal Blackheath Golf Club were afterwards entertained at dinner by the Members of the London Scottish Golf Club at the Dog and Fox, Wimbledon, Lord Elcho in the chair.'

On 15 March 1870 Blackheath were hosts in a foursome match with ten pairs a side. Blackheath were again the victors, winning every match but one, and by 40 holes to 3. Since Blackheath had been playing the game since the seventeenth century it is hardly surprising they should be victorious in these early matches; but their Wimbledon rivals were learning fast. In May 1870, on a fine warm day at Wimbledon, with the ground very hard, the home team lost by only 11 to 9, with one match halved, or by 54 to 48 holes. This match, like the earlier matches, was played over three rounds of the seven-hole Common Course.

Perhaps stung by these successive defeats the Committee made a special effort for the 1871 match, when Blackheath were challenged to a 20-a-side contest, two long rounds, again counting holes. There was to be practice every night in the first two weeks of May, when the Professional Tom Dunn would fix up games and no doubt weigh up form. The team on this occasion would be chosen by the Captain on the basis of the cards returned. This preparation paid off. On 16 May – 'a fine day, ground very keen' – came Wimbledon's first victory by 10-8, 42 holes to 35; but next year Wimbledon were routed at Blackheath – so badly that the score was not recorded in the Club Minutes. In 1873 the Blackheath Match took place at Wimbledon in the middle of the Spring Meeting. It was to be singles, 20-a-side, but only eighteen Blackheath men made the journey to Wimbledon. After 16 matches it was still all square – still counting holes – but the Wimbledon's last two representatives were 1 and 7 up respectively giving the home team victory by 8 holes.

This match occasioned a letter to *The Field*, when a correspondent wrote: 'We seldom get accounts of great matches played at Blackheath or Wimbledon. Anxiously expecting the result of one to be played between these two Clubs on the 21st by twenty redoubtable Blackheath knights of the hickory against twenty of the London Scottish on their own crowing heap, we have heard by a side wind that the Blackheath lost by 8 holes . . . Possibly the men in dark clothes in the business metropolis, who look so grave in the grand offices around the Bank of England, would not like it to be known, more than the MP who is on the Committee of the House, that they spend the afternoon or all day upon the Links playing golf. It is surely an excusable liberty to take with business, and a great mistake to think that golf interferes with work . . . If clients, customers, and constituents would only prove that what adds to health adds to length of life, and length of life to experience, they would be only too glad to learn that absence in a cause which would bring the principal back with renewed vigour was doing good to them all'. A truly admirable philosophy, which can be echoed today.

On the same day there was a match between the two Club Professionals, Dunn of Wimbledon and Bob Kirk of Blackheath, which the former won by 1 hole. 'Some uncommonly fine golf was exhibited on both sides.'

An interesting match was played on the Wimbledon Course in 1877 when Tom Dunn challenged the former Open Champion, Tom Morris, who had been attending the Autumn Meeting at Westward Ho!, over 36 holes. The month was October when 'Golf reigns again in full force at Wimbledon, and players are drawing home from other greens to settle down, after some grumbling, to what is not, they soon acknowledge, so bad a green after all'. The chosen day 'dawned on a steady downpour of the finest and most penetrating rain . . . It was a bad prospect for play. However, the Club officials were early on the spot and a select body of keen golfers were prepared to watch the combatants'. In those leisured days *The Field* found it possible to record every shot played by the two men – 367 of them; but here we can afford to describe only a few holes.

At half-past eleven Tom Morris struck off, taking 'the honorary lead accorded to veterans. [He was 66.] The ball was well struck, but the line taken rather to the right of the true one – a fault on the right side in more senses than one. Dunn followed suit in the same direction', and thanks to local knowledge won the hole. Then both 'addressed themselves to the first ravine. The hole is now very long, the tee having been placed twenty yards to the left, behind the curling pond, and the putting green in the old place beyond the seat. Dunn set his opponent a good example by a long shot well in the line, and Tom followed suit with an equally good one. Dunn's second placed him on the green – Scylla and Charybdis, thornbush and rushbed, being skilfully lofted. Morris, who played a full shot instead of a three-quarter one, slightly pulling his ball, and getting a forward fall to the left, disappeared amid the foliage of the glen. This, of course, was fatal, and though after lifting he made a good bid with his iron for the hole, it fell to the younger player at four to six.

'The Third hole was approached in a cautious fashion on both sides, both playing well to the left to avoid the hollow. Old Tom was again too gentle with his putts, not realizing how spongy Wimbledon is on a wet day; and in the result three up for Dunn was recorded. It was evident that all the resources of the veteran would be taxed to reduce this lead, as Dunn was playing in fine form, and the day made local knowledge specially important'.

In the course of the match the two men lost shots in bushes, bracken, rushes, water, and of course the beloved whins, illustrating the difficulty posed by the early Common Course, even for the Professionals. At the end of the first round 'the home hole presented an uncheerful vista, its obstacles looming gigantic in the rain' but Dunn found himself four up. 'After an adjournment, during which the candidates and their admirers endeavoured to place themselves more in rapport with the moist atmosphere [a delicate way of saying that libations were poured at the Nineteenth Hole], the little band cheerfully started for the second round.' Morris came back strongly. At the Eleventh in spite of lying among stones 'he played with his long spoon what was certainly the shot of the day, and reminded one of the spectators of a shot of the same kind, and by the same player, at St Andrews, which he has not forgotten for ten years'. At the heathery hole, the Fourteenth, 'Morris chose the better line, Dunn being rather too ambitious of a straight one, and being up in two while Dunn was short, seemed to have the inside turn; but his putt being for the first time off the line, a half in five was decisive against the match being pulled out of the fire. Dormy four on the two rounds, after a fine fight in the second. The next hole settled the question, being taken well by Dunn in three to five'. Dunn was round in 91 and 89. Morris in 94 and 93.

Several of the early Oxford v. Cambridge matches were played on the Common Course. The Conservators were upset when someone – no doubt an anti-golfer – drew their attention to a report in the local press in 1880 'that the inter-University match was to be played by the kind permission of the London Scottish Golf Club' and instructed their Clerk to write to the Club demanding an explanation. Having thus indicated their displeasure, they agreed that the match should go ahead. It was the custom to entertain the teams to lunch in the Clubhouse, which led to some internal friction. Alexander Davidson, one of the two brothers who presented the Silver Shield, was a painfully law-abiding citizen. He discovered that the undergraduates, deeming their hosts' hospitality to be marginally short of perfection, were paying for drinks out of their own pockets. He believed this was infringing the food and drink laws, which was confirmed by the Club's Treasurer. He took it upon himself to save the fair name of the Club, and a possible appearance in Court, by paying visitors' drinks bill, which came to £3. Seemingly a modest sum but then representing 360 glasses of Scotch, enough, one might imagine, to drown the sorrows of several defeated undergraduate golf teams.

The self-righteous Davidson, no doubt of Scottish extraction, then sent the bill to the Club, and asked to be reimbursed. The Committee were highly displeased by his initiative, although one Member thought he might have a point. It would be disastrous if a technical infringement of the law deprived the Club of alcohol for all time. It was concluded that the Member's 'interference was quite unnecessary, and indeed to be regretted. The custom of the Club that visitors introduced for a week were entitled to all privileges ... was good enough to meet the case now, as in many years past'. Nevertheless the £3 would be refunded – but it was not to be a precedent.

The Committee said as much when they sent Davidson a cheque, which he 'declined to accept on account of the Committee's expressions'. He threatened to submit the case to the Inland Revenue's District Officer; but was persuaded to descend from his high horse and let the matter drop. It was decided that the visiting teams would continue to be temporary members entitled to pay for their own food and drink, whatever Mr Davidson and the Inland Revenue might think. Happily the law no longer casts doubt on the propriety of our visitors standing themselves a modest half pint – or even more.

The new Course in 1907 was brought into play without ceremony, but when it was redesigned in 1924 the opening was marked by a match between the Club and the Oxford and Cambridge Golfing Society. 'Colonel Malcolm [then Captain] started proceedings by declaring the Course open for play, and himself formally struck the first ball. The caddies, it was observed, had contended for presumably profitable pitches on the right near the wood.' They guessed wrong, for the Captain hooked his shot over the trees to the left. 'The reward for retrieving it therefore went to an optimist who had posted himself in the dim distance, and when he arrived at the teeing ground panting from his furlong sprint, he turned out to be a total stranger' – no doubt to the fury of the regular caddies.

Nor did the match itself go according to plan. Roger Wethered, chosen to lead the Society's team, came from Scotland, but his train was four hours late and he missed the morning singles, which the Club won 6-5. The man Wethered was due to play (V. A. Pollock) was beaten on the last green by the better ball of two substitutes (in spite of his valiant attempts to talk them out of the match), but 'the officers of the RWGC obstinately declined to let the meritorious performance of Wethered's substitutes count'. Since the overall result of the legitimate singles and the foursomes (in which Wethered played and lost) was 8½ points each, 'the match was, in the opinion of the hosts, halved. Their guests will always maintain that they won it'.

Although the match was a light-hearted affair, as befitted the occasion, some of the golf was outstanding. The top Society pair (Wethered and G. L. Mellin) were 2 up with 3 to play, having, for example, had a 3 at the 455 yards second which they reached with a drive and a mashie. But their Wimbledon opponents (F. S. Bond and G. F. Girdlestone) finished brilliantly, winning the 390 yards Sixteenth with a 3, the short Seventeenth with a 2, and the final hole (380 yards) with a 3.

Royal Wimbledon play a limited number of inter-club matches, in the interest of Members who play at weekends: against Royal Blackheath (dating from 1867), Oxford, Cambridge, the Oxford and Cambridge Golfing Society, Surrey County, and Woking. Domestic matches include the Men's and Ladies' matches against the Artisans, and Men against the Ladies, all pleasant social occasions rather than bitterly contested encounters. There is also a 5-a-side Men v. Ladies match without benefit of handicap, a triangular match with the Club's neighbours, the London Scottish and Wimbledon Common Golf Clubs, and an annual match with the All England Lawn Tennis Club.

In 1927 the Club subscribed to the *Golf Illustrated* fund 'for the purpose of sending a number of British Professionals to America . . . to compete in the US Open Championship, and to take part in the first official annual international "Ryder Cup" match against the American Professionals' at Worcester, Mass. (which the United States won 9-2, with one match halved. Britain had earlier won unofficial matches at Gleneagles in 1921, and Wentworth in 1926).

FROM THE RWGC COLLECTION

Gutty Ball, c. 1890 (left); **1924 Dunlop Maxfli** used by Colonel Malcolm to open 1924 Course (centre); **rubbercore ball** c. 1906 (right). (See page 137.)

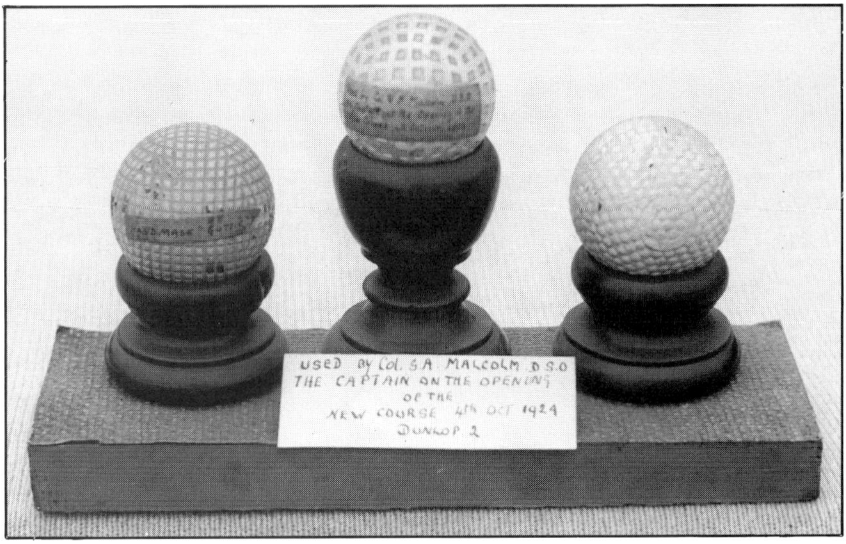

Sixteen

LADIES

THE MINUTES OF THE LONDON SCOTTISH record on 6 April 1872 the rules of the Wimbledon Ladies' Golf Club. Although the Club is so described, its official designation is 'The Ladies London Scottish Golf Club'. The London Scottish rules apply 'except as to Subscription, the Committee, and Dress'. The care of the Course and ajudication of disputes is left to the men who will be Honorary Members. The Annual General Meeting will be as near St Andrew's Day as convenient. The Honorary Secretary is Marianne Holland. In January 1875 the Conservators were told that the Ladies' Club, an adjunct of the Men's, had 14 Members, all but two from Wimbledon ratepaying families. The following year the men presented the Ladies with a trophy, a gold cross set with pearls, later referred to (with a hint of regret) as a heavy expense. The last winner was Henry Lamb's sister, and when the Ladies' Club ceased to function in 1879 she was allowed to keep it.

In March 1884 Norman Foster, Secretary of Royal Wimbledon, proposed reviving the Club but failed to generate enthusiasm. In October the Captain, Guy Pym, became the Ladies' champion. The resuscitation of the Club was discussed 'at considerable length' (perhaps a euphemism for 'with considerable heat') and it was left to him to make proposals. 'Again owing to a great diversity of opinion among the Members so much time was occupied that finally the matter had to be dropped ...' The Ladies' Club was filibustered to one side.

In October 1890 Ethel Few (presumably a low-handicap player) asked the Conservators for permission to form a Course on the Common; but 'found some difficulty in making the necessary arrangements'. Some gentlemen 'better able to carry out the desire of the Ladies' took over. Led by Laidlaw Purves, they announced in the local press and to Members of Royal Wimbledon and London Scottish that the Club was to be revived and invited applications for membership. 145 ladies, and 23 men (offered associate membership) showed interest. Members of the original Club were invited to join, without entrance fee, and 6 accepted. Miss Emily Pearson sent in the original Members' list. The first Minute Book turned up later so that the Minutes of the last General Meeting (February 1878) could be confirmed by the first of the new Club. Those Minutes are concerned mainly with competitions, recording, for example, the 1878 February medal, won by Issette Pearson with gross 68.

The Conservators were sympathetic and allotted ground for a new nine-hole Course west of the Long Range Butts. They were assured by the Ladies' Committee (at first all men) that the beauty of the area would be enhanced by levelling the now disused Butts. Elsewhere the ground would be left in its natural state. The linings of the holes, four inches in diameter, would be 'of the Bembridge pattern'. The First, Third, Seventh, and Ninth flags would be red; the others, white, except the Fifth, red and white. Laidlaw Purves helped with a constitution and rules. 'The St Andrews Rules' were adopted except that three of his – a stroke penalty instead of loss of hole for lifting from a hazard, hitting the ball twice, and dropping a club length from any paling, ditch, old rifle butt, or enclosure – were preferred. Play days were to be Tuesdays, Thursdays and Saturdays. Associate men must play with a lady, and only associates on the Committee could enter the Clubhouse, Thatched Cottage, leased from the Conservators. The caddies' fee was fixed at 3d. for 9 holes, a penny less than the price of tea, bread and butter. A short list of suitable Latin mottoes was drawn up.

In spite of a nine-week frost when work had to be suspended, the Course was ready in May 1891. It was laid out 'in a manner which had given satisfaction to the Ladies and with a minimum of inconvenience to other persons using the Common'. A map deposited at Manor Cottage, the Conservators' headquarters, no longer survives. A lady who knew the best Courses in Britain wrote: 'I consider this one of the most difficult as there is not one hole without bunkers or whins between the tee and the green; and as a bye-law for the protection of whins prevents a ball being played unless it can be done without hitting the whin, it is seldom that a round is completed without one or two lifts'. The holes ranged from 127 to 207 yards, the total for the nine holes being 1420 yards.

William and Annie Frost of 28 Crooked Billet, Wimbledon, were hired as caretakers at Thatched Cottage: 'Me and my wife will be pleased to take your ingagement . . . and will a Greed to your ingagement letters and will do our best to please'. It was intended to employ a Professional and a Greenkeeper, to allow the former to concentrate on club-making and teaching. The Committee promised to find an apprentice who had just served his time. All things being equal, an English Professional was to be preferred to a Scot.

The Greenkeeper, Weston, was quickly found. He was asked to repair clubs until a Professional was appointed but proved unsatisfactory. In November 1892 the Committee told him he 'could do well enough if he liked' but he did not mend his ways. The Royal Wimbledon Professional, David Patrick, was therefore asked to send over an apprentice on play days to do repairs, sell clubs and balls, and manage the caddies – all profitable business. Weston was left with unremunerative chores: looking after the Course, cleaning the closets, lighting the workshop fire, opening the Ladies' lockers, keeping the hole pots and flag sticks in good repair. When he heard this news he gave a group of Ladies a piece of his mind, and affixed to the notice board 'a sort of proclamation addressed to Members'. He was given a week's wages in lieu of notice, and five minutes to get off the premises.

When the Club still failed to find a Professional, Patrick sent 'a respectable caddy, able to teach', on Tuesdays. The Club paid him 2s.6d. a day, and his pupils paid 1s.0d. for nine holes instruction. In 1899 Roland Jones gave the Ladies lessons. Later the same year Frost, who must have shown some aptitude for golf, was given a chance to act as Greenkeeper/Professional at 15s.0d. a week, being provided with a machine for reconstituting balls. In 1901 he was also given charge of the Clubhouse garden and allowed to teach 'when his green work allowed it', for which he had an extra 5s.0d. a week.

The Ladies, who had so humbly believed the men were better qualified to relaunch the Club, may have doubted their judgement. Thatched Cottage was very dilapidated. The men, having repapered it, floored and match-boarded the stable, installed a new lavatory, and made other structural improvements, decided it must be rebuilt. An architect was called in, plans submitted to the Conservators, and duly approved. Rebuilding was completed in September 1891. When the Conservators found the Cottage was 4 feet higher than authorized they insisted that 4 feet must be lopped off, in spite of the great cost. Further, they had asked that the thatch be replaced with Staffordshire tiles. Those selected were deemed to be too garish for the staid Common, and must be darkened.

When the Club became operational in May 1891 beginners among the Members were issued with 'A Description of the Game', and urged to master the rules. Couples must have at least one marker, over 15 years old, not a relative, and approved by the Committee. The definition of 'a relative' caused difficulty; and it was sensibly decided that all players might mark each other's card regardless of ties of blood. Those bringing guests were reminded that 'it entails much delay for opponents to borrow each other's clubs'.

An inaugural 'Prize Meeting' was held in June 1891. Three classes were planned: scratch to handicap 4; 5 to 12; and 13 to 18, Members being allowed to choose their class, a generous provision swiftly withdrawn. Instead handicaps were established through two competitions in May, played in the three classes. However, since only five players won handicaps of 4 or better 'it was ordered that there should be two classes: 0 to 18; and 19 to 36'. In the inaugural Meeting, however, there was no class distinction. Maybe there should have been. The prize winners all played off long handicaps: 22, 29, 36, and 34, which produced nett 73, 74, 74, and 77, leaving the better players nowhere. In the Meeting in 1892 there were two classes, 0 to 24, and 25 to 36, played on different days, the lower class marking for the higher on one day, and vice versa on the other. A special plea was made to the Ladies to have their carriages wait on the road by the Fifth green. At the Clubhouse the horses

Thatched Cottage, the first Ladies' Clubhouse, which still stands on Wimbledon Common.

would be in the line of play to the Fourth hole; and at the Fifth tee they would be in danger from the Royal Wimbledon Second hole. The Ladies were more compassionate than the men, who in announcing results to the sporting press did not spare players with 140 or worse. The Ladies merely recorded 'there were several players over 100'. In 1899 the Club decided to conform to the LGU handicapping practice.

In December 1891 Laidlaw Purves, always striving for scientific perfection, provided the Ladies with a handicapping scheme: 'the following being the salient features of its working: handicaps to be regulated on the scratch of 37 and 74 taking the best 4 rounds of nine holes – if less than 10 returns of nine holes, a penalty of a stroke, a penalty of a stroke for each nine holes short of ten. A further penalty of a stroke for each win up to 3. Less than 3 returns to be handicapped arbitrarily'. If these were the salient features, the small print must have been mind-boggling.

The men continued to look after the Club – its finance, rules, handicaps, Course, and relations with the Conservators – until 1893. The Ladies merely managed the domestic business of the Clubhouse, keeping in touch with the men through correspondence. That they were grateful for their help is witnessed by a presentation to Franklin Adams, Secretary to the Men's Committee, which deeply touched him; but in April 1893 (perhaps influenced by the mess the men had made over the Clubhouse) they said they were now experienced in club management. 'Should it meet with your approval we shall be glad to undertake more responsibility ...' – to arrange matches, tell the Handicap Committee about form, have money to buy prizes, receive Associate Members in the Clubhouse, and subscribe to *The Queen*, *Gentlewoman*, and

Members of Wimbledon Ladies' Golf Club outside Thatched Cottage in the 1890s.

kindred periodicals. The men agreed about matches, handicaps, and periodicals, but not about prize money, or men in the Clubhouse.

Laidlaw Purves could not stand idly by. He demanded equal representation for the Ladies on the Committee – more than they had asked for. When he persisted the Committee transferred their powers to a General Meeting, a move which some Members saw as sinister. The Meeting was a shambles, in which the Chairman was shouted down. Franklin Adams explained in a circular that their objective was to allow the whole Club to decide its future; and it was given a second chance to do so at the Annual General Meeting in June.

Proceedings now became farcical. The Committee resigned en bloc before the AGM, except that Franklin Adams agreed to act as Secretary during the Meeting. To demonstrate impartiality the Committee submitted three mutually exclusive resolutions: that Ladies should have sole management; that the men should carry on unchanged; and that the Committee should be fifty-fifty. A group of Ladies demanded the removal of four named men from the Committee. Franklin Adams asked for a poll of all Members. An associate wanted a Committee of five Ladies and two associates. Mr Cumming Macdona MP, always in favour of women's lib., suggested the Ladies should manage their own affairs, but elect a men's committee as a court of appeal. Six Ladies and four men were nominated to fill the vacuum left by the resignation of the men's Committee.

The vast agenda was dominated by Laidlaw Purves's contribution – a massive resolution proposing seventeen complicated changes in the rules which reads like the Committee stage of a major parliamentary bill. His main proposal was a 13-member Committee with nine Ladies. There is no record of the AGM but the resolution that the Committee should comprise six women and four men triumphed; and with the passage of time men played a smaller part in Committee business.

Franklin Adams were big enough to give the Ladies the benefit of his advice before severing his connection with them. He confirmed that the last recorded General Meeting of the original Ladies' Club had been held in February 1878, and that in November 1879 he had been handed their remaining assets – £2.0s.6d. in a pink bag. £2 had been used to pay a debt, but he had retained the 6d. ever since, and now handed it over. He warned that turf must be bought as thick as possible, never rolled up, because the Common soil was so shallow. Great discretion was needed in rolling the greens – the mowing machines as a rule did all that was required. Don't save the greens for medal days – it does them good to be walked on. Had the new Conservators been well-disposed he had intended to ask for ground to the north-east of the Sixth and Seventh holes, between these holes and the road running north north east to the Windmill, to extend the Course. They might do a deal with the Conservators about laying on water to some of the greens. As to the Professional: 'Patronage in the way of club-making, buying balls, and playing, wants to be looked after, or our present arrangement will fall through'. He had intended when a second Lady Captain was elected to propose that Captains' portraits in uniform frames should be hung in the Clubhouse. He advised against hiring married couples as servants – two replacements would be needed when they resigned. Finally, he provided sketches showing how the Clubhouse might be enlarged.

In the early days the Club boasted many of the best players in the country. Their team was said to be 'almost invincible' and many Members distinguished themselves in the Ladies' Championship, which Lena Thomson, daughter of Robert Thomson, one of the founders of the Ladies' Club, won in 1898. She had learned the game 'almost as soon as she could walk', at North Berwick, Leven, and St Andrews. These players were immortalized by the poetico-journalists of the day:

The famous Lena, have you seen her
  Deadly short approaches?
When these you see, you will agree
  This golfer Tom Dunn coaches.

and of course Issette Pearson

The Wimbledon pet is Miss Issette

Although she was not a Member, one distinguished Wimbledonian cannot be omitted from this Golden Treasury of Verse:

> Now Lottie Dod, so neatly shod,
> Stands forth upon the tee.
> On tennis green she is the queen,
> At golf what shall we see?

Like the men, most Ladies belonged to several Clubs. Agnes Tyrwhitt-Drake, for example, Captain in 1894–95, was also a member of Eastbourne, North Warwickshire, and North Berwick.

The Ladies continued to manage their affairs with success. They made Laidlaw Purves a Life Member, and later his wife and daughters were similarly honoured. In 1899 an extension of the Course to make two really long holes by playing 'over the ravine and over and beyond the old butts' was approved by the Conservators. Frost was given a bonus of 10s.0d. in acknowledgement of his help in retrieving balls from water, and £1 'to replace boots worn out in our service'. Mrs Frost was allowed to stock clubs for sale in a corner of the Clubhouse. In 1905 a telephone was installed. Medal mementoes were ordered from Mr Halfhide of Wimbledon. Dogs were banned from the Clubhouse, but men were at last allowed in. The Club gave loyal support to the Ladies' Golf Union, which Issette Pearson had helped to found.

The Minutes of this time reflect a relatively untroubled existence. Dealings with the Conservators were cordial. Requests for modifications to the Course were acceded to without argument. A new green was made with its own water supply; fences were built to protect the whins so dear to the heart of the men and trees were planted. The Conservators graciously allowed the Ladies to remove the cesspool from their garden, provided they promised to return it if called on to do so. They undertook to take action against loafers making a nuisance of themselves near the Clubhouse. Applications to play on the Ladies' Course by men who were not associates (no doubt because they believed the Common was free for all without regard to sex) were politely refused by the Conservators. They explained that the Course had been established for the use of ladies 'and it was thought desirable to keep it for that purpose'. Equally when the Ladies asked permission to play on the men's Course unaccompanied by a man they were told the Conservators did not see their way to change the regulations.

The Ladies' Club's relations with Royal Wimbledon were equally cordial. They were allowed to use the men's Course for a tournament in 1896, when the men volunteered the courtesy of the Clubhouse as well. However, when Cumming Macdona later brought two ladies to lunch and tea, there was trouble. Professor Lankester was outraged and immediately reported the gross breach of the rules. Macdona, unrepentant, refused to apologize, and tried to exploit the situation. He drew the attention of the Conservators to this discrimination and even went so far as to ask them 'to make it compulsory for the Club to open its doors to ladies, provided extra days of play were granted'.

In June 1908 when it was understood that Royal Wimbledon might want to dispose of 50 acres of the land they had acquired to build their new Course the Ladies were tempted to take them over to make a second nine-hole Course. Nothing came of the idea, and a plan to enlarge the Clubhouse was substituted, and approved by the Conservators.

In 1909 the Ladies Club joined with Royal Wimbledon, London Scottish, and the newly-formed Town Golf Club in protesting to the First Commissioner of Works about proposed new bye-laws for golf on the Common. (See Chapter 4: *Conservators.*) In 1914 the Club again asked Royal Wimbledon for a lease of part of Warren Farm to make a golf course; but they had missed the

Issette Pearson, founder Member of Wimbledon Ladies' Golf Club, and the Ladies Golf Union.

Lena Thomson, English Ladies' Champion, 1898.

bus. The transfer of the lease was already being negotiated with Middlesex County Council.

Gertrude Tee, seemingly of sterner stuff than Ethel Few, was a notable champion of the Ladies' cause. She made several applications in 1912 and 1913 for permission to add another nine holes to the Course, all of which were refused. The Conservators did examine the proposals, but thought they would cause great inconvenience to the public. One of the few discordant notes in this period was struck by a resident of Putney who complained to the Conservators that his daughter 'had resorted to the Ladies' Course to practice golf' only to be told by the ground man and a Lady Member that she had no right to be there. A caddy contributed his quota of abuse. His daughter was also reprimanded for making a tee with sand belonging to the club by the same Lady Member who said resignedly one could not stop thieves from thieving. The complainant was told that the Ladies' Club had gone too far. They would be taken to task by the Chairman of the Conservators. The Ladies claimed the girl had flouted the rules and etiquette of the game and deserved all she got; but nevertheless they reminded Members that the general public had every right to play on their Course. So long as they behaved properly they must be unmolested.

When the Course was taken over to make an army camp in 1915 the Ladies asked for access to the men's Course for the duration, unaccompanied by a man, proposing that only those with handicap 15 or lower should play. The Conservators referred the request to Royal Wimbledon, still entitled to use the Common, although they were beginning to question the value of the privilege, having now their own Course. They in turn referred it to the Joint Green Committee with the London Scottish. Eventually the Conservators ruled against change. With commendable gallantry, and after much debate, Royal Wimbledon in September 1915 admitted ladies to their new Course, for as long as they were dispossessed by the camp, not an easy decision. The cost of providing accommodation for Lady Members – even without the necessary furniture – was estimated at £120.

Stiff conditions were laid down. The Ladies' Club would pay £150 a year, and pro rata in the year when the war ended. They would be allowed to use the Course on Mondays, Wednesdays and Fridays, except on public holidays and competition days. They could not hold their own competitions, nor would they have the privilege of introducing guests. They could start only before 9.30 am or after 10.30 am; and no Lady's ball or that of a Member playing with a Lady was to be 'put down on the starting board' between those hours. They must wear their Club badge when playing. Caddies would not be provided before 10.30 am. The Professional would not be allowed to teach them on the Course. Finally, the rules of golf, the etiquette of golf, and the bye-laws of Royal Wimbledon must be strictly observed. The Ladies were of course highly delighted. The Secretary was instructed to send off a cheque for £150 immediately, perhaps in case the men should change their minds, and to express the Club's appreciation of the great courtesy shown. Club badges were hastily ordered; and rooms were found at 11 North View where the owner, Mrs Gardener, undertook to supply food.

When the rank and file of Royal Wimbledon were told what was in the wind there were some who disapproved. After all they had been a gentlemen's Club for more than half a century. The proposed invasion of privacy was more than one infuriated back bencher could take. He wrote to the Committee about 'a certain resolution' – it was too shame-making to quote the wording – that had been passed. 'As neither the Committee nor the gentleman who thought fit to have this resolution placed on the agenda had the courage to put their names to it, and for other reasons, I am inclined to dispute the validity of the resolution *in toto* as affecting the existing rules and regulations of the Club.' He demanded to see the Committee Minutes, so that he might study the resolution, if indeed it was a resolution. The Committee side-stepped this assault. Their most tactful member was deputed to take the aggrieved gentleman on one side and 'settle the matter in an amicable manner'. This was statesmanlike for the Committee had been by no means unanimous in welcoming the Ladies Club. The tactful Committeeman accomplished his mission and there was no further protest.

The General Meeting agreed the Ladies should come in on the terms proposed. That they were without a Course was due to the fortunes of war and no doubt some of the men realized that if the War Office had requisitioned their Course the boot could easily have been on the other foot. They might have found themselves begging for the right to play on the Ladies'. In December 1917 J. L. Ridpath went over the top. He proposed that ladies should be admitted to the Club on the same terms as men, and went so far as to suggest the writing room become the Ladies Club Room, that suitable dressing room accommodation be provided, and that the Ladies be admitted to the Dining Room for luncheon. 'The Royal Wimbledon Golf Club, gratefully appreciating the splendid self-denial of the Ladies in doing their bit in the war, invite them to become Members on the same terms and conditions as the men.'

The Committee were startled; and this time the Captain was deputed to put Ridpath back on the rails. They proposed to allow the Ladies to play five days a week instead of three, and to introduce lady friends. In the face of these concessions surely there was no need to proceed with his drastic motion? Ridpath accepted this, and in April 1917 the new arrangements were brought in. The green fee for a lady's guest was fixed at 1s.0d., the same guest not to be introduced more than six times a year. The Ladies had to agree in writing that lady guests introduced by Members of Royal Wimbledon could use their Club rooms.

At the Spring General Meeting in 1919 further concessions were made, apparently without argument. The Ladies were allowed to hold a medal competition on the third Wednesday of the month when they could start up to 10 am, instead of 9.30, the only proviso being that they must give way if they held up a men's match. They were also allowed to hold their own Spring and Autumn Meetings. When they held a special meeting in December – consisting of a round in the morning, and a putting competition in the afternoon – they were allowed to start at any time. It might seem that there was no limit to the courtesy of the men; but in January 1920 when they agreed the Ladies might leave their cars in the garage, it was only if the men did not require all the available space.

Norman Foster, who had served the Club ably as Honorary Secretary and had been elected Captain in 1906, was well disposed towards the Ladies, ahead of his time. In February 1920 he wrote to the Committee, heading his letter 'Ladies Question Again', and putting forward proposals which went even further than Ridpath's in 1917. He pointed out that the Ladies had in 1915 been allowed to use Royal Wimbledon 'for the duration of the war', later amended to 'during such time as the Ladies' Course is occupied as a Camp'. There seemed to be no immediate prospect of the camp's closing and he suggested that the Ladies' 'security of playing privileges be extended to the end of our lease in 1932, subject to any unforeseen circumstances which would reasonably revoke the privilege'. He also asked that they should be given permission to erect their own Clubhouse near the Curling Pond (now the car park). Foster, with his long experience of the affairs of the Club, knew that he must carry the Committee with him, and asked what they thought. They were not to be drawn. They regretted that they were unable to express an opinion.

The Ladies Club was expected to help to meet the increased cost of maintaining the Course, more than doubled since 1915. In June 1920 they agreed to raise their contribution to £250; and also to double the green fee for visitors to 2s.6d. The War Losses Commission made it easier for them to meet their liabilities by granting them £65 a year from the date in 1915 when the Course had been taken over until the military authorities ceased to occupy it. By 1921 the Ladies seemed to have become a permanent feature. They were given, *nem. con.*, permission to hold their Spring Meeting and use the Putting Green. Competitors might start at any time. Further, they were licensed to play seven-a-side matches for the Pearson Cup starting at 2 pm on days to be fixed. Equally, when the time came for the Autumn meeting, there were no problems. It seemed that the men had become accustomed to their face.

In February 1922, when the army had folded their tents and disappeared from Wimbledon Common the Ladies wrote to Royal Wimbledon acknowledging their agreement was due to terminate and enquiring whether they might carry on their privileges. Financial considerations ruled out rebuilding their own Course and they suggested a meeting to discuss the future. Royal Wimbledon replied that a meeting was pointless. This was something of a brushoff but the men then appointed a sub-committee to consider the matter. A memorandum set out dispassionately the arguments for and against continuing the arrangements. The Ladies caused extra wear and tear to the Course but it could stand it; and their annual payment was enough to provide the labour and materials needed to keep the Course in good order.

The memorandum was sent to 573 Members accompanied by a ballot paper asking 'Should the Ladies' Club continue to play on the Royal Wimbledon Course?' to which 305 Members answered 'Yes' and 93 'No'. 185 were in favour of five playing days for Ladies, 108 for four days, and 109 for three days. On the basis of this evidence it was decided that the Ladies should continue to use the Course, but only on Mondays, Tuesdays, Wednesdays and Fridays, except public holidays and competition days. They would contribute £300 a year; their number would be limited to 200; and in electing new members they would give priority to the wives, daughters or sisters of Members of Royal Wimbledon. The Ladies were sternly reminded that the rules and etiquette of golf, and the local rules of Royal Wimbledon, must be strictly observed. They humbly thanked their brethren for 'the continued privilege of the use of the Links', making no protest at the loss of Thursday as a playing day. All these arrangements were to be subject to one year's notice.

In September 1923 this notice was given, why is not clear. The arrangements were working smoothly – the Ladies had regularly held their competitions, and there is no evidence that they had failed to observe the rules and etiquette of golf. Equally wrapped in mystery is the reason for reversing the decision. The notice to quit is recorded without comment in the Minutes of the Ladies' Club on 26 September 1923, which suggests that it caused no alarm or despondency; and the next communication from the men is a letter in December saying it is proposed to raise the Ladies' contribution to £500 a year. It may have occurred even to those gentlemen who fought to keep the Ladies out in 1915 that they were worth their weight in gold, if nothing else.

The Ladies seem to have been as little moved by the increased contribution as by the notice to quit. As it would mean increasing the subscription to £4.4s.0d., they suggested it was reasonable to allow them to play five days a week. This was agreed, and for the next eight years it was business as usual, the Ladies being given permission to hold their various annual competitions, and to use the Course for matches, including those for the Pearson Trophy. If anything the men became more favourably disposed. They agreed that their female relatives should no longer have priority in the matter of election to membership, but only in three cases out of four. Many of the rank and file, however, took a different view. In May 1928 40 asked for the termination of the agreement with the Ladies, ostensibly because their presence midweek hindered work on the Course and kept it from getting the necessary rest. When three years later 30 men asked that the Ladies should be allowed to lunch in the Club there was fierce opposition.

In 1932 there was a major step forward. It was agreed the Clubs should amalgamate, the Ladies having five-day membership. They would contribute £500, thereafter individuals would pay an annual subscription of £7.7s.0d. The Ladies agreed, and met the Captain (Mr G. H. Sim) and Secretary (Captain Tippet) to discuss details. The £500 was considered reasonable, since the Clubhouse would have to be altered. Royal Wimbledon would be responsible only for finance and catering. The Ladies would have their own Committee and elect their own Members. There was a problem, however.

They had no power to amalgamate. They had to change their constitution to enable the Club 'to be dissolved, or wound up, or amalgamated, with any other Golf Club at such time and upon such terms as shall be approved by a majority of Members voting at a General Meeting'; and to accept the offer of amalgamation. This done, the representatives of the two Clubs finalized the arrangements. The Ladies' Clubhouse on the Common would be closed after the next Autumn Meeting. The Ladies' Committee would have their own Honorary Secretary. Separate Members' lists and local rules would be printed. Much time was devoted to discussing meal prices. Tea, bread and butter, an indicator of the economy both national and Royal Wimbledon, was fixed at 6d.; three course lunch, 3s.6d.; fish lunch, 2s.0d. 'If a member brings her own food, 9d. table money will be charged.' Would men be allowed to use the new lounge? '... although one did not wish to be inhospitable ... there should be one room for ladies alone.' A separate entrance by the caddies' yard was objected to. It should be by the Professional's shop.

The last General Meeting of the Wimbledon Ladies Golf Club was held on 15 November 1932 when it was resolved 'That the ... Club dissolve and that the Members ... be now Five-day Members of the Royal Wimbledon Golf Club'. A photograph, which it was suggested 'would look better if golf clothes were worn' was taken to mark the historic occasion. The stage was set for the equally historic first meeting – on 25 November 1932 – of the Committee of the Ladies' Section of Royal Wimbledon Golf Club. It was devoted to tying up loose ends. Might the Ladies' spend small amounts of Royal Wimbledon money? Might they have a clock and a fire guard in their Lounge? A small sum for flowers? The Men's Committee graciously acceded to all requests. However, when in May 1934 21 men suggested the Ladies should be allowed to use the Clubhouse at weekends the Committee took refuge in the fact that it would need a change in the rules, call for more staff, and an extension to the Club premises.

From this time until the outbreak of World War II there was no change in the constitution of the Ladies' Section. Spring and Autumn Meetings were organized, the usual competitions were held, the Section played a part in the administration of Surrey County golf, and in the affairs of the Ladies' Golf Union. In 1938 they proposed that Members who had joined in 1914 or earlier, and who could no longer play, should become Non-Playing Members at a reduced subscription. The Men's Committee agreed but then changed their minds. The time was not opportune.

In October 1939 the men agreed that ladies on national service unable to play during the week should play at weekends after 11 am and 3 pm. Wives of Members accompanied by their husbands could play at the same times on payment of a green fee. The Ladies accepted this with gratitude, realizing it 'would be withdrawn on the proclamation of peace'. In October 1945, some weeks after the war ended on VJ Day, they tactfully wrote to the Men's Committee recording their appreciation of the weekend facilities enjoyed for six years; and the men agreed they should continue for the time being.

At the end of June 1945 an Extraordinary Meeting of the men authorized the Ladies Section to nominate up to 50 weekend members (increased to 65 in 1957). In 1951 when it was pointed out that 'many Members would like to be allowed to bring their wives, daughters, or friends into the Clubhouse on Saturdays and Sundays, rather than that they should have to wait in their cars outside' the men were sympathetic. The greatest breakthrough came in 1953 when a referendum produced a majority of more than two-thirds of the men in favour of allowing the Dining Room to be mixed, albeit with separate tables for ladies. There followed a chain reaction in which the Ladies' dining room became a second billiard room, and the snack bar became a mixed bar. The Ladies deprecated the loss of their own dining room, since their accommodation was restricted, and the only access to the mixed Dining Room was along the verandah; but they gave way gracefully, perhaps still savouring their escape from purdah (see p. 82) which allowed them, as they consumed their roast and two veg., to see and be seen by men.

No Member of the Club has won the English Championship since Lena Thomson's success in 1898; but Royal Wimbledon teams have continued to distinguish themselves in competitions. The Pearson Trophy, founded by Issette Pearson for teams of seven with handicaps of 13 to 30, and played for by Clubs in Surrey, Kent, Herts, and Middlesex, was won by the Royal Wimbledon in 1983, and in 1984 they were runners-up. The Club won the Hicks knockout competition for teams of five playing off scratch, also in 1983, and were runners-up in the following year. The Surrey Scratch Foursomes competition for a trophy presented by Molly Gourlay, was won in 1982 by Marina Penna and Rosemary Roberts. The Sunningdale Ladies' Foursomes, started between the wars by the Ladies' Golf Magazine *Fairway & Hazard*, has had many Royal Wimbledon finalists; but in 1980 all four finalists came from the Club. Jill Martyn and Diana Dixon beat Ann Rutherford and Liz Phillips four and three. The Club won the Kingswood Salver – an invitation event organized by the Kingswood Golf Club for teams of three Silver and Bronze pairs – in 1978 and 1984, and were runners-up in 1985.

The record for the Ladies' Course was broken in the Autumn Meeting, 1978, by Ann Rutherford with 72, and equalled in 1985 by Brigitte Wilenkin in the October Medal. Their cards read as follows:

R = Rutherford **W** = Wilenkin

Hole	*Yards*	*Par*	**R**	**W**	*Hole*	*Yards*	*Par*	**R**	**W**
1	348	4	4	6	10	442	5	5	5
2	395	4	4	4	11	376	4	5	5
3	320	4	5	4	12	408	5	4	5
4	363	4	4	4	13	132	3	2	3
5	135	3	2	3	14	418	5	4	4
6	224	4	3	3	15	322	4	5	4
7	459	5	4	4	16	357	4	5	4
8	143	3	4	3	17	115	3	3	3
9	260	4	4	4	18	304	4	5	4
		35	34	35			37	38	37

The Ladies' Section celebrated their Centenary on 18 July 1972, with a twelve-hole Stableford foursomes competition, for which the weather was as kind as it had been for the men's Centenary competition seven years earlier. It was distinguished by a hole in one at the Eighth by Nellie Bryan. Lunch, to which all former Members were invited, was held in a marquee in front of the Clubhouse, when to commemorate the occasion the Men's Captain (Commander James Allan) presented a Silver Salver which is now played for annually in the June Medal. After lunch Barbara Dowling and Ann Draffin, dressed in the latest fashion of 1872, complete with outsize hats, and using clubs and balls of the period, drove in the new century.

Seventeen

SUGGESTIONS

THE SUGGESTION BOOK is the key to the successful administration of every Golf Club, the safety valve of the pressure cooker, enabling the aggrieved Member (and who has never had a grievance?) to let off steam without bursting. It allows him to think he has made an intelligent contribution. It enables those in command to keep a finger on the pulse of their troops, and to consider remedial action. The operative words are 'to consider'. There is no guarantee that anything will be done. All the suggestions in all the suggestion books in all the Golf Clubs in Britain acted upon in a normal year can be recorded on the average score card.

The Complaints and Suggestion Book of Royal Wimbledon Golf Club is no exception although it has been more relaxed than the national standard. This claim may be disputed; but an annual average of 6.48 entries over the past quarter century – about one every two months – seems moderate. Even the 12.25 annual average of the 1920s is not excessive. 1962 and 1983 were golden years – not a single suggestion, although the Suggestion Book may then have been missing, thereby frustrating its suggested replacement. Those items recorded in the lifetime of the Club provide evidence that human nature is unchanging, and that history repeats itself in Golf Clubs no less than in the narrower outside world.

As to history repeating itself:

November 1921	Will the Committee consider what steps can be taken to prevent Members removing papers, periodicals and magazines from the Drawing Room?
September 1926	Books, magazines, and papers are continually removed from the Drawing Room.
October 1930	*Punch* ... found it missing twice in ten days.

and so it has gone on to the present day, and will go on to the end of time. Frustrated readers had other grievances:

July 1937 That those Members who indulge in the hobby of solving crossword puzzles should be requested to bring their own newspapers with them for that purpose and not use the Club papers to the inconvenience of other Members who require them for reading and reference.

Chess players were just as much at risk:

October 1936 The set of black and yellow chessmen belonging to the Club had disappeared since the close of last season. Could it be found, please?

October 1938 That an enquiry be made as to the whereabouts of the Club chessboard, and that the Member responsible for removing it from the Drawing Room be asked to return it immediately.

Less supple members had their own problems:

April 1969 Can we have some long shoe horns in the changing rooms? For the particular benefit of older Members.

December 1973 Could shoe horns please be provided for the changing rooms?

A recurrent theme is the contest between the run of mill Members who play the game at weekends for exercise to recharge their run-down batteries for another wearing week in the City, and the elite who carry the banner of the Club into contests with rival Clubs, and the lesser elite who do battle for the traditional Monthly Medal:

June 1922 If it is thought desirable to play inter-club matches on Saturdays it is submitted that even in summer they should start before 10 am. Today ordinary Members have been practically deprived of their enjoyment of the Links until 11.30 which is unfair.

October 1927 The undersigned wish to protest against Club matches being played on Saturdays during the winter months, when the number of Members, mostly limited to weekends, who wish to go round is as large as the Course can carry without the addition of strangers.

February 1936 With reference to the rules now in force regarding order of play on Medal Days, and in view of the fact that less than 10% of the Members of the Club avail themselves of these privileges – may I suggest that the majority who come to the Club for an enjoyable day's golf may be given a great deal more consideration?

World War II brought a *cri de coeur* from a Member who had occasional problems with bunker shots:

September 1944 Owing to the difficulty in purchasing new golf balls it is suggested that in the event of a new ball having been played into a bunker the player may replace it with an old ball – Apologies for pencil, which leads to the complaint that no pen is available in the Drawing Room.

October 1961 What about some new furniture for the Smoking Room? And some ink! [Pencil entry.]

October 1963 There is no ink, no writing paper, and the handles are off two drawers.

January 1930 That the three ancient balls in the case above the mantelpiece in the Drawing Room wilfully overthrown by some sacrilegious hand, be restored to their rightful position.

October 1949 It is observed that the sacrilegious hand, dormant for many years, has struck again.

November 1956 It is to be regretted that the advent of card players to the Drawing Room has seemingly brought about another overthrow of our ancient golf balls in their glass case. We respectfully refer to Pages 143 and 279 of this book.

September 1967 In former years complaint by a Member was justifiably laid against the overthrow of three ancient golf balls that had stood, possibly since the institution of the Club, on perches inside a glass case on the mantelpiece in the Drawing Room, and as a result such a sacrilegious act was quickly righted. Now both the glass case and the three ancient balls have entirely disappeared. Can they please be restored to their rightful and honoured positions in the Clubhouse?

– It is much regretted that the present whereabouts of the case and golf balls is unknown ie they are lost.

– Found, 17.10.67.

The catering services are a fairly regular target:

September 1932 The draft [sic] bitter beer is very unpalatable. I found it impossible to drink a half tankard to the end.

June 1936 The Club cheese is not what it was.

May 1952 That something be done to ensure that the supply of ice is equal to the demand in hot weather.

June 1952 No ice at 6 pm.
Still no ice at 1.30 pm or 6 pm.

November 1952 That the specific gravity of afternoon tea be doubled.

March 1963 May the Club Wine List please be brought up to date? A few days ago I entertained guests from Muirfield offering them with some pride Crofts 1927. The wine turned out to be Crofts 1945, a great port as is known, but the equivalent of a generation adrift.

October 1965 The rolls at lunch today were very stale.

From a fair weather golfer:

November 1945 As the weather in the northern hemisphere is slowly but surely deteriorating as the years go by, it is suggested that at the weekends an up-to-date met. report be placed on the Club notice board.

A reminder that a Golf Course is a living organism susceptible to change:

February 1935 That, for the benefit of those golfers who hit their tee shots with a shade of fade, an implement be provided for retrieving golf balls from the pond at the Thirteenth.

A double disaster suffered by one gentleman Member:

January 1968 No Club Stilton. Females at every table.

It seems that 1968 was not a vintage year for the Ladies Section:

May 1968 In view of the present climate prevailing in the Club, may we suggest that Ranson's Cottage be converted to the Ladies' Club House?

Nor was the next generation popular:

April 1969 On Good Friday there was a baby-in-arms on the verandah. Today there was a baby in a pram. Why is this permitted?

On the other hand:

February 1981 We wish to suggest for the Committee's consideration that Ladies should be permitted the use of the Men's Lounge and Bar daily after 5.30 pm during the winter months.

Finally, the perfect illustration of the therapeutic value of the Complaints and Suggestions Book, and of the stout defence put up against it by those in authority:

October 1968 It would enable Members to read the Club Notices if the odd table under the Notice Board were removed. I have suggested this to Captains, Secretaries, and Committees for the past 13 or 14 years without success. Is this Table a Holy Cow?

[It was.] "The Committee has decided that the Table shall remain where it stands."

The Ladies must have the last word – if only because they have preserved their original Suggestion Book, whereas the Men's was last heard of being hawked along the Portobello Road. It runs from 1891 to 1983, but with considerable gaps. The very first suggestion, on 10 November 1891, is the provision of 'a Cloathes Brush for the Ladies' Room', which was approved, as was a request for a 'hand glass'. A later plea for 'a long glass to see petticoats' was firmly rejected. 'There is no room for anything of the kind.' Miss Gedge asked that soap should not be 'scrub floor'. A proposal for a Club ribbon was enthusiastically taken up. Miss Thomson suggested black, red and white; Miss Scott preferred black, white and red; Miss Phillips, black and red; Mrs Jolliffe, dark green and red; and Mrs Dowson, pale blue, red and black. Miss Agnes Tyrwhitt-Drake's proposal for a Club Button was approved. Miss Frere's suggestion that there should be a Club Coat – red, with black collar and cuffs piped with white – was accepted, and it was recommended that black skirts and hats should be worn with it.

Suggestions that the holes should be named – 'Sleepy Hollow', 'Homeward Bound', 'Switchback', 'The Rubicon', for example, seem not to have met with favour. Mrs Alexander King's criticism of the state of the tees was considered fair by Franklin Adams. It might be necessary to make wooden tee shots compulsory on the long holes. In the autumn of 1895 the tees were so muddy that it was suggested to use boards covered with canvas. A proposal to alter the Ninth green by filling in a 'Valley of Sin' was ruled out on the ground that the improved turf now made it possible to putt from the valley. The caddy problem is reflected in a number of suggestions. They should be required to wear badges and their names and addresses should be taken by Weston so that they could be disciplined.

Thatched Cottage was the target of numerous suggestions. A proposal that the main room should have a separate entrance, so that men could use the Clubhouse, was turned down by Franklin Adams. An umbrella stand was provided without argument. There was more difficulty over a hat rack. 'Having been so generous as to give us something on which to hang our hats, the Committee might ask for subscriptions towards supplying hooks instead of nails. By way of a start I hope they will accept the following' – one halfpenny. Mrs Cundell asked that the notice board should be lowered, which it was – to a position where it could not be read without the reader's dress being scorched by the fire. A proposal for a ping pong table generated the reply 'Under no circumstances whatever'. Bridge was more favourably dealt with. It was agreed that it should be played in the Committee Room, with stakes limited to a shilling a hundred – the inflation conversion is left to the reader's imagination.

Food caused the Ladies fewer problems than it did the men. Someone asked that fresh halfpenny buns should replace the stale cakes being served. The provision of ice for 'the lemonade and such like drinks' was suggested in June 1893. 'Miss Scott suggests that when it is impossible to know beforehand that a chop will be required for luncheon, and that one is brought up as the only alternative of letting Mrs Frost know, a more reasonable charge than 9d. should be made for cooking same. 4d. or 6d. should be ample.' The advantages of economy of scale did not escape Issette Pearson when she dealt with this complaint. 'The charge for cooking a chop has been 6d. The charge of 9d. included 2d. for potatoes and 1d. bread. As the cooking and serving of a chop entails considerable labour, this charge is not considered too much, but two chops together would be done for less.'

Dare we look into the Suggestion Book of the future?

June 2201 Update history of Club.

January 2286 Extend Course lease to February 2586.

Appendices

PRESIDENTS

1865	Lt.Col. Lord Elcho
1878	Lt.Col. Henry Lumsden
1882	The Rt.Hon. The Earl of Stair
1885	The Rt.Hon. The Earl of Elgin
1888–94	The Rt.Hon. The Lord Kinnaird
1908–19	The Rt.Hon. The Lord Rathmore
1919–29	The Rt.Hon. Viscount Finlay
1931–35	HRH The Prince of Wales KG

VICE-PRESIDENTS

1908–16	The Rt.Hon. The Earl of Mexborough
1919–27	Capt. The Hon. Reginald A. R. Plunkett-Ernle-Erle-Drax DSO RN

CAPTAINS

1865–68	A. G. Mackenzie Esq.
1868–70	Dr R. E. Dudgeon
1870–72	R. Henry Usher Esq.
1872–74	William Porteous Esq.
1874–75	John Anderson Esq.
1876–78	J. M. Collyer Esq.
1878–80	Col. Geo. H. Moncrieff
1881–82	Robert A. Deane Esq.
1882–83	Lt.Col. E. H. Kennard
1883–84	John Taylor Esq.
1884–85	Guy Pym Esq.
1885–86	John Murray Esq.
1886–87	Edward Sidgwick Esq.
1887–88	J. Lionel Ridpath Esq.
1888–89	Alex. Davidson Esq.
1889–90	W. R. Anderson Esq.
1890–91	Henry Lamb Esq.
1891–92	W. C. Anderson Esq.
1892–93	A. Chivas Adam Esq.
1893–94	Sir W. Style Bt.
1894–95	Sir Alexander Moncrieff CB
1895–96	H. Seton-Karr Esq. MP
1896–97	Sir R. B. Finlay QC SG
1897–98	Dr W. Laidlaw Purves
1898–99	John Ferrier Esq.
1899–1900	J. R. Dunlop Hill Esq.
1900–01	H. P. Cumming Esq.
1901–02	Robert Thomson Esq.
1902–03	F. J. Walker Esq.
1903–04	H. Howard Batten Esq.
1904–05	Sir Westby B. Perceval KCMG
1905–06	R. H. Pringle Esq.
1906–07	Norman R. Foster Esq.
1907–08	F. Beckett Birt Esq.

1908–09	A. G. Rickards Esq. KC
1909–10	Wm. Muir Esq.
1910–11	J. Cornock Taylor Esq.
1911–12	Sir Thomas R. Hughes KC
1912–13	Sir James Devonshire
1913–14	Sir Charles Tyrrell Giles KC
1914–15	Edward Tanner Esq.
1915–16	F. S. Cresswell Esq.
1916–18	Arthur Carr Esq.
1918–19	William Higgins Esq.
1919–20	Stephen Fairbairn Esq.
1920–21	C. Murray Smith Esq.
1921–22	Brig.Gen. Sir David Kinloch Bt. CB MVO
1922–23	Col. G. A. Malcolm DSO
1924–26	Sir Joseph Hood Bt.
1926–27	Gen. Sir Malcolm H. S. Grover KCB KCIE
1927–28	Dr R. Worth OBE
1928–29	HRH The Prince of Wales KG
1929–30	A. R. Faulkner Esq.
1930–31	F. W. Brown Esq.
1931–32	G. H. Sim Esq.
1932–33	Lt.Col. A. L. Foster
1933–34	W. R. Rumbold Esq. MC
1934–37	R. Y. Sketch Esq.
1937–38	Philip Carr Esq.
1938–39	R. H. Pavitt Esq. MC
1939–43	Col. C. M. Croft DL JP
1943–44	S. Hill Esq.
1944–45	Dr D. H. Anthony
1945–46	F. S. Gentle Esq.
1946–47	H. W. Hern Esq.
1947–48	Ernest Cornwall Esq.
1948–49	W. J. B. Horne Esq.
1949–50	A. M. Macdonald Esq.
1950–51	Horace R. Hern Esq. DFC
1951–52	L. N. Rawes Esq.
1952–53	Dr Gordon Hodgson
1953–54	E. L. Clarke Esq.
1954–55	E. C. Millard Esq.
1955–56	D. Overall Esq. JP
1956–57	N. W. Clarke Esq. MC
1957–58	G. C. Killick Esq.
1958–59	H. Seys-Phillips Esq.
1959–60	Leslie Williams Esq.
1960–61	F. H. Cassells Esq.
1961–62	A. L. Smith Esq.
1962–63	E. B. Dixon Esq.
1963–64	C. F. Tyler Esq.
1964–65	W. Lister Barber Esq.
1965–66	Sir J. E. Cradock-Hartopp Bt.
1966–67	F. W. Barnes Esq.
1967–68	Lt.Col. W. H. Hutton MC
1968–69	Dr S. Cochrane Shanks CBE
1969–70	A. R. Brackenridge Esq.
1970–71	A. R. Pike Esq.
1971–72	Cmdr. J. C. Allan
1972–73	P. M. Kelly Esq.
1973–74	The Hon. Sir John Stocker
1974–75	E. Scudamore Esq.
1975–76	A. M. Hendry Esq. TD JP
1976–77	H. L. Riseley Esq.
1977–78	J. Fracis Esq. MC
1978–79	Frank Denny Esq.
1979–80	Sir Martin Flett KCB
1980–81	Ian M. Bowie Esq.
1981–82	David Evans Esq.
1982–83	David Cornock Taylor Esq.
1983–84	John Bevan Esq.
1984–85	Stanley Harding Esq.
1985–86	The Hon. Sir Barry Sheen

CAPTAINS OF THE LADIES' SECTION

1892	Miss Issette Pearson
1893	Miss L. Thomson
1894	Miss A. Tyrwhitt-Drake
1895	Miss A. King
1896	Mrs Willock
1897	Mrs Dowson
1898	Miss Issette Pearson
1899	Miss A. Tyrwhitt-Drake

1900	Mrs Cameron
1901	Mrs Willock
1902	Miss H. M. Frere
1903	Miss Maclean
1904	Mrs Norman Foster
1905	Miss H. A. Macfarlan
1906	Mrs Horace Martin
1907	Miss Berton
1908	Mrs F. W. Brown
1909	Mrs Lyndhurst Towne
1910	Miss Q. Macintyre
1911	Mrs Hannaford
1912	Mrs Eustace White
1913	Miss H. A. Macfarlan
1914–20	Mrs F. W. Brown
1921	Mrs Eustace White
1922	Mrs E. T. Bolton
1923	Miss Benton
1924	Mrs Rackham
1925	Miss G. M. Pavitt
1926	Miss E. M. Archer
1927	Mrs Newcombe
1928	Miss Benton
1929	Mrs Eustace White
1930	Miss Leslie Brown
1931	Mrs John Bates
1932	Mrs R. Worth
1933	Mrs Eustace White
1934	Miss H. Joannides
1935–36	Miss J. McLintock
1937	Mrs D. C. Arnell
1938	Mrs H. D. Ellis
1939–46	Miss J. Stewart
1947–48	Mrs D. C. Arnell
1949	Miss H. Joannides
1950	Miss R. Duff
1951	Mrs H. D. Ellis
1952	Mrs K. M. Turner
1953	Mrs W. A. Young
1954	Mrs M. Pearse
1955	Mrs C. Whitmore
1956	Mrs H. Seys-Phillips
1957	Mrs A. M. Hendry
1958	Mrs E. C. Tyrwhitt-Drake
1959	Mrs C. Rutherford
1960	Mrs E. G. Benn
1961	Mrs H. K. Hardcastle
1962	Mrs E. C. Millard
1963	Mrs R. K. Graham
1964	Mrs C. K. S. Aylwin
1965	Lady Bateson
1966	Mrs T. R. A. Bevan
1967	Mrs H. D. Ellis
1968	Mrs E. H. Fryer
1969	Mrs T. A. Hussey
1970	Mrs M. M. Denny
1971	Mrs D. C. Arnell
1972	Mrs R. F. Phillips
1973	Mrs K. Onwood
1974	Mrs B. C. Sheen
1975	Mrs G. Dunbar CBE
1976	Mrs M. Cruickshank
1977	Mrs D. L. Evans
1978	Mrs F. W. Byrne
1979	Mrs A. F. Whitfield
1980	Mrs M. Heaton
1981	Mrs R. D. Fox
1982	Mrs A. M. Hendry
1983	Mrs P. Harvey
1984	Mrs C. E. Messent
1985	Mrs B. Edwards
1986	Mrs A. Crowhurst

SECRETARIES

1869–71	Captain Wm. Porteous
1872–75	John Grant Esq.
1876	J. M. Collyer Esq.
1877	W. Walker Esq.
1877–90	Henry Lamb Esq.
1890–1900	Norman Foster Esq.
1900–03	R. Peirce Esq.
1903–06	W. T. Hughes Esq.
1906–21	Captain W. H. Hutson
1922	W. T. Hughes Esq.
1923–27	Lt.Col. R. F. Walters
1927–28	Major K. A. McRea

1928–37 Captain H. C. C. Tippett MC
1937–38 Captain G. N. Openshaw
1939–45 R. A. Leppingwell Esq.
1945–60 Captain G. N. Openshaw
1960–68 Edward Scudamore Esq.
1968 E. C. Millard Esq.
1968–70 Brigadier R. Davenport OBE
1970–71 L. S. Foster Esq.
1971 H. K. Shersby Esq.
1972–78 Commander Guy Harris
1978 H. K. Shersby Esq.
1979– Major George Jones

PROFESSIONALS

1865–70 Doleman
1870–81 Tom Dunn
1881–86 John Thomson
1886–91 Alexander Patrick
1891–96 David Patrick
1896–99 J. H. Taylor
1899–1900 Peter Paxton
1900–02 R. Fullarton
1902–07 R. Munro
1907–11 Roland Jones
1911–12 Ben Sayers Jr.
1912–26 Jack Fulford
1926–50 Fred Leach
1950–52 Alan Dailey
1952–83 Russell Dailey
1983– Hugh Boyle

BLUES

Oxford

1889, 1890, 1891 J. W. B. Pease
1904 G. R. Girdlestone
1920 R. R. Burton
1920, 1921 R. H. Wethered
1947, 1948 A. G. B. Helm
1958 N. A. J. Winter
1960, 1961, 1962 N. M. Stephens
1970, 1971 S. C. Butt
1970, 1971, 1972 J. P. Turnbull
1973, 1974 S. M. Turnbull

Cambridge

1889, 1890 H. S. Colt
1895, 1896, 1897 Bernard Darwin
1911, 1912 H. Gardiner Hill
1912, 1913 C. Gardiner Hill
1921, 1922 J. A. Bott
1932 F. A. Simmonds
1935 G. O. Peake
1946, 1947, 1948, 1949 A. J. Weir
1953, 1954 O. J. Whitmore
1954, 1955, 1956 R. Q. O'Brien
1956 B. H. Longrigg
1961, 1962, 1963 R. J. Bevan
1968, 1969, 1970 A. D. Swanston
1974, 1975, 1976 C. E. Travers
1978, 1979, 1980 P. Green

ROYAL WIMBLEDON GOLF COURSE 1907-1924

(showing earlier holes superimposed on present-day course)

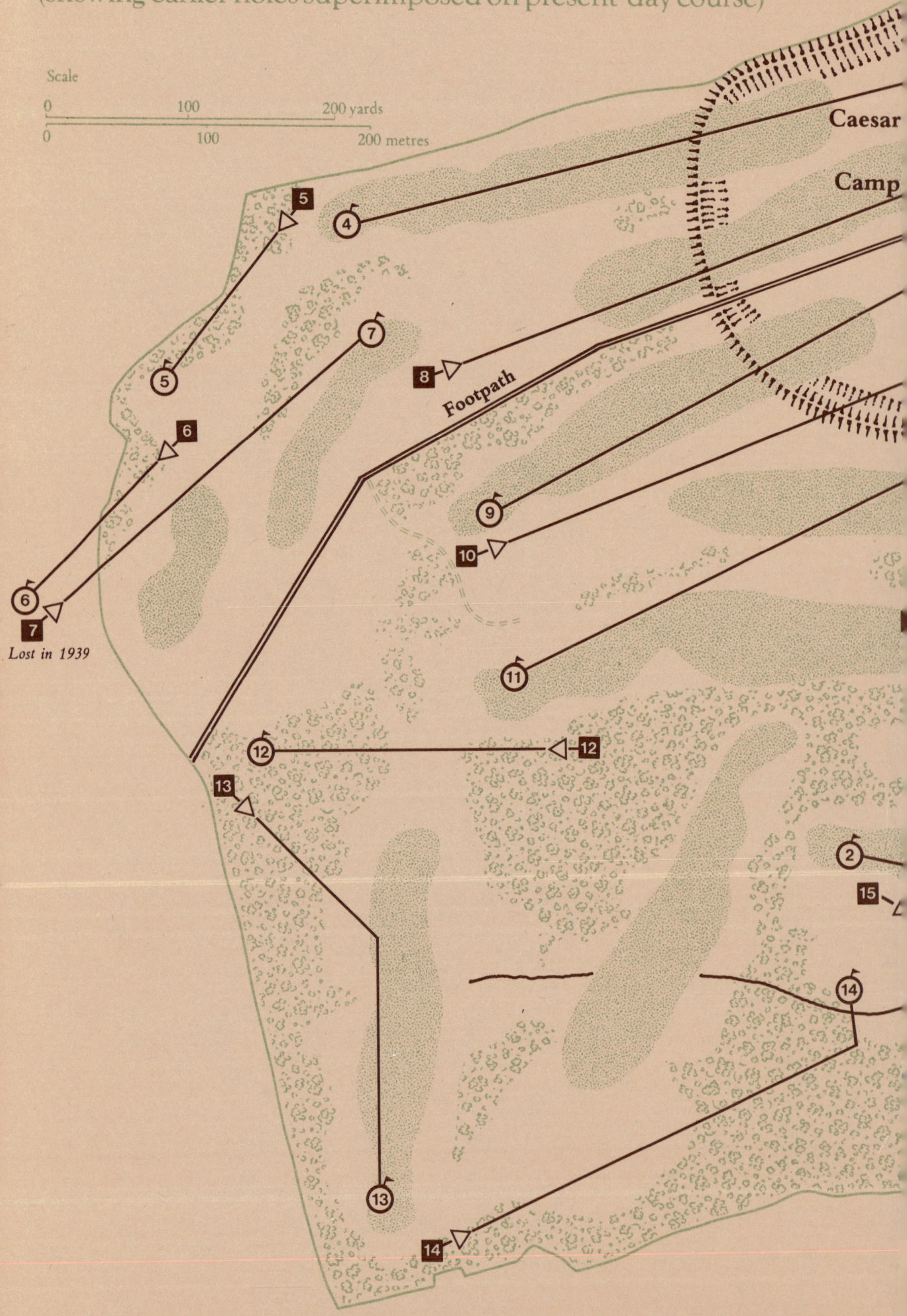